READ UP

VOLUME 2

DESCRIPTIONS AND DISCUSSION QUESTIONS FOR MORE THAN 30 THOUGHTFUL BOOKS

FOREWORD BY

C. CHRISTOPHER SMITH

InterVarsity Press
Heart. Soul. Mind. Strength.

InterVarsity Press
P.O. Box 1400, Downers Grove, IL 60515-1426
World Wide Web: www.ivpress.com
Email: email@ivpress.com

InterVarsity Press® is the book-publishing division of InterVarsity Christian Fellowship/USA®, a movement of students and faculty active on campus at hundreds of universities, colleges and schools of nursing in the United States of America, and a member movement of the International Fellowship of Evangelical Students. For information about local and regional activities, write Public Relations Dept., InterVarsity Christian Fellowship/USA, 6400 Schroeder Rd., P.O. Box 7895, Madison, WI 53707-7895, or visit the IVCF website at www.intervarsity.org.

Labyrinth photo on p. 82: Dan Gill

Cover design: David Fassett
Interior design: Beth McGill
Images: © Lasse Kristensen/Getty Images

ISBN 978-0-8308-5789-0 (print)
ISBN 978-0-8308-9886-2 (digital)

Printed in the United States of America 0

green press INITIATIVE InterVarsity Press is committed to protecting the environment and to the responsible use of natural resources. As a member of Green Press Initiative we use recycled paper whenever possible. To learn more about the Green Press Initiative, visit www.greenpressinitiative.org.

P 15 14 13 12 11 10 9 8 7 6 5 4 3 2 1
Y 22 21 20 19 18 17 16 15

CONTENTS

THANK YOU!

Reading for pleasure and reading for learning involve a different sort of attention but both are mostly for benefit of self. Reading in order to create discussion questions is something entirely different. As soon as something really gets your interest and you want to read fast—you need to slow down, stop and figure out what's the question that will bring about the discussion that's at the heart of this passage, this chapter or this book.

I'm grateful to the many colleagues and friends that joined in the work of creating the discussion questions you find here. Among them are Adrianna Wright, Alisse Wissman, Ashley Davila, David Fassett, Diana Verhagen, Jon Boyd, Karli Saner, Lisa Renninger, Michelle Graham, Nicole Spewak, Rebecca Carhart, Sarah Johnson and Stephanie Jewell. Without their collaboration I'm certain a *Read Up, Volume 2* would not exist.

Thank you for stopping in your reading in order to cull together questions that begin conversations. Your contribution will benefit readers like you and me—walking and talking together on faith and in faith.

Read Up!

Lorraine Caulton

Lorraine Caulton

Foreword by . . . C. Christopher Smith

By all indications, North Americans in the twenty-first century are reading more than we ever have, but the ways in which we are reading are shifting dramatically. We are reading faster and tending to focus on shorter pieces like those found on blogs, Facebook or Twitter (with its 140 character limit). With billions of books and articles available to us at any time through a few taps of our fingertips on our smartphones, it is no wonder we tend to read frantically. This sort of fast reading, like fast food, may help us meet some short-term goals as individuals, but generally speaking it does not help us to be more attentive to our neighbors and to the realities of the places we inhabit.

It is not surprising then that in the last few years a Slow Reading movement has arisen—one of a growing number of Slow movements including Slow Food, Slow Money, Slow Cities and others—that challenges us to read slowly, attentively and in ways that help to cultivate deeper and more sustainable communities. Slow reading, however, should not be unfamiliar to us in the Christian tradition, as we have many historical practices of reading Scripture slowly and carefully, such as *lectio divina* and even preaching. Although Scripture is the shared story at the heart of our life together as the church and we should never cease studying it, we also need to be reading and talking about other books in our churches, books that help us understand the world in which we live and how we are to dwell faithfully in it.

In our age in which it is rapidly becoming a lost art, the importance of ***conversation*** should not be overlooked. It is in conversation that our ideas and languages and dreams get forged into common structures that shape the life of our communities—church, neighborhood, workplace, etc. Perhaps the most important thing our churches can do today is to develop habits of conversation with one another and with our neighbors, in which we can know and be known, and out of which we are ever learning to care better for one another and for our places. Reading is a sort of fuel for these conversations, providing energy in the form of words and ideas that bring life to and clarify our conversations.

The book that you hold in your hands—be it in print or in digital format—is a wonderful conversation starter. Not only does it recommend some really good and timely books, at least some of which will be pertinent to the shared life of your church, it also highlights some questions about these books that will surely get your conversation rolling. I pray that this little volume will stir up many conversations, leading you into more questions, but ultimately into deeper and richer faithfulness in your local church communities.

C. Christopher Smith, author of *Reading for the Common Good* (forthcoming) and coauthor of *Slow Church: Cultivating Community in the Patient Way of Jesus*

"If we encounter a man of rare intellect,
we should ask him what books he reads."

Ralph Waldo Emerson

ADVENTURE OF ASCENT

Field Notes from a Lifelong Journey

Luci Shaw

For most of us, growing older is a reality we put off as long as possible—until we realize with a shock that it is happening to us. We immediately look around to see how others on the path just ahead of us are dealing with it. So here is the intrepid writer-poet Luci Shaw, taking readers on a virtual hike with her, with steps more deliberate and slow but also with surprising vistas that fill us with gratitude.

Luci has given us a lifetime of exquisite reflections on nature, love, death, suffering, loss, faith, doubt, creativity, curiosity, lifelong learning—all of it drawn from the breadth of her own experience, harvested in penetrating and lyrical insights. Still active in her eighties, Luci now turns her attention to the season of edging toward the borders, serving as a fearless and eloquent scout. These field notes will inform your own journey, no matter what your age.

"Luci keeps her face turned to the beauty of Christ and shows us all how to climb, handsomely and with dignity. Wise, strengthening, playful and loving."

Emilie Griffin, author of *Green Leaves for Later Years*

"I love this sage book."

Lauren Winner, author of *Still*

ABOUT THE AUTHOR: Luci Shaw is a poet, essayist, lecturer and writer-in-residence at Regent College, Vancouver. She coauthored three books with Madeleine L'Engle and is a founding member of the Chrysostom Society of Christian Writers. Her books include *Breath for the Bones: Art, Imagination & Spirit*, *Harvesting Fog* and a collection of her poems, *Scape*.

◆ QUESTIONS

1. Author Luci Shaw writes poetically about her "lifelong journey." What are you feeling as you begin this discussion on aging?
2. "Our expressions vary; some have a grin for anyone who greets them; some project enthusiasm and optimism; some faces are drawn with effort and ache" (p. 16). What expression would people say your face conveys now? How do you expect it will change—or do you expect it to change—in the future?
3. Aging brings physical limitations and diminished mental capacity. Do you fear physical or mental losses more? What in particular?
4. Luci shares that driving frees her from the hindrances of physical disability (p. 25). What new activities have you found that reduce the inevitable limitations due to aging?
5. Why do you think we as a society are so fixated on aging, or preventing aging?

   "I struggle with ambition, the hope that something I've contributed to the world has lasting value, and might even be unique, what no one else has done or could have done" (p. 53). Do you think it's a realistic goal to live life with no regrets? Why or why not?
6. Luci talks about "a good death" (p. 63). Have you witnessed such a passing? What would it look like to you?
7. Luci shares her experience of being treated as "a fragile old lady" (p. 65). When have you experienced a similar feeling? If you are younger, does her story affect how you might treat those older than you?
8. In chapter 9, Luci shares what brings her comfort and rest: a warm bed, music, beautiful scenes from Christmas cards, poetry, nature and prayer. What brings you comfort, or is this something you need to discover in your life?
9. Throughout the book Luci brings up the question, "What is the significance of the present moment when the rest of life looks so drastically limited?" (p. 157). What is your answer to this question?
10. Luci's elegant style of writing offers up many soulful nuggets. Which in particular were meaningful to you?

Excerpt from . . . **Adventure of Ascent**

I see us wherever I go. The ones who are old enough to be full of the accumulated wisdom and insight of a rich lifetime. The ones whose faces still betray a certain confidence and fortitude. The ones who continue to have optimism about the future of the human race, and hope still to contribute to it. And the ones who have gone blank; who are saying to themselves, *What's the use?* (Though that's not a question; it's more a statement of reality.) These are the ones who don't have the energy to care anymore. It makes me wonder: is there a difference between acceptance (*It is what it is. Live with it*) and passivity (*I just can't be bothered anymore*)?

We are an aging population, and we crowd the malls and the churches and the supermarkets and airports and streets. We look for elevators instead of stairways. We get around in wheelchairs, or scooter chairs, or the special carts the supermarkets provide for the disabled (after surgery I've used them, and they work well enough, allowing some mobility for the ordinaries of living). If we can still pass our driving test and take to the road, we drive a bit more cautiously and hang our blue-and-white handicapped placard from our rearview mirror to claim the reserved spaces in the parking lot. There seem to be more and more such spaces allotted for our use. For them, too, I am grateful.

I've learned to take my placard with me when I travel, so that if I rent a car in some other city I can use it. I watch for those special parking spots with their blue-and-white signs. They mean that I won't have to walk so far to get to some entrance, some destination.

We are bent and slow, and our gait is often constricted by pain. We get the AARP bulletin in the mail that gives us advice about how to perk up our sex life and deal with the social security crisis. Though demographics show that we are achieving political power, weakness, slowness and caution have begun to characterize our movements. We plod. You could call our speed deliberate, because we almost have to *deliberate* before mounting the next step. Some of us are accompanied on our grocery outings—perhaps a younger woman, a graying spouse, an equally frail friend, or just our own cane as a companion.

Our expressions vary; some have a grin for anyone who greets them; some project enthusiasm and optimism; some faces are drawn with effort and ache. The expressions of some seem to define what loneliness looks like. A kind of interior resignation etches many features. From the language of the body I translate it as *What else can I do?* We keep going. It's our only option.

Like the smoke that pollutes the sky somewhere
I'm a dream that dissolves in endless air.
So why should I care that I'm losing my hair?

When I see this kind of shriveling in another human being, I automatically straighten up, walk taller and try to pull in my stomach. It's a sign to myself that I haven't given up yet. My mother had a thing about good posture, and I was well-trained, made to walk around the house balancing a book on my head, which requires a truly vertical spine. Mother lived to ninety-nine, though against her iron will arthritis eventually curled her into a human comma.

I used to be proud of myself that I could run up and down a flight of stairs. My father raced, *two steps* at a time, up any staircase he encountered around the world until he was over eighty. Perhaps for both of us it was a kind of showing off, a bravado, a way of defying the odds, of proving that disability hadn't caught up with us. Yet. I'm still in a house with stairs. I take a nap in the afternoon. My study is on the ground floor, but having our bedroom upstairs means I must make several climbs a day to the second floor. I tell myself it keeps me mobile.

It hurts a lot, especially my left knee, which has only recently been "replaced" like its right counterpart. It doesn't want to bend much, so it hurts even more coming down the stairs, even though gravity is on my side. Tylenol for Arthritis is my constant friend.

But it was Emerson who said: "People do not *grow* old. When they cease to grow they *become* old."

ANXIOUS

Choosing Faith in a World of Worry

Amy Simpson

Our culture is frantic with worry, but we are called to live and think differently from the worried world around us. The fact is, worry is sin, but we don't seem to take it seriously.

How can we live life abundantly, with joy, as God has called us to do, when we're consumed by anxiety? Challenging the idolatrous underpinnings of worry, Amy Simpson encourages us to root our faith in who God is, not in our own willpower. We are commanded not to worry, and the Bible makes it clear that the future belongs only to God. To live with joy and contentment, trusting God with the present and the future, is a countercultural feat that can be accomplished only through him.

"As fascinating as it is funny, as convicting as it is clever, Anxious *gives us a gander into Jesus' mind and what he must've been thinking when he said, 'Do not worry.'"*

Caryn Rivadeneira, author of *Broke*

"[Amy] helps us understand that it's far more effective to address worry as a problem with the way we think, rooted in what we believe about God. Here's the good news: there is hope for all of us worried people, and it's found in faith."

Anita Lustrea, host of *Midday Connection*

ABOUT THE AUTHOR: Amy Simpson is a former publishing executive and award-winning author who currently serves as editor of Christianity Today's Gifted for Leadership and senior editor of Leadership Journal. She has written numerous resources for Christian ministry and is the author of *Troubled Minds: Mental Illness and the Church's Mission.*

Visit Amy's website and read her blog at amysimpsononline.com.

◆ QUESTIONS

1. Before reading this book, did you think that you struggled with worry? Do you tend to under- or over-emphasize worry?
2. Amy suggests that our culture has a hierarchy of sins (p. 11). Where do you think worry falls on the scale?
3. According to the introduction, what is the relationship between fear, anxiety and worry?
4. Telling the story about her encounter with a moose, Amy states, "the fear response is not only necessary—it's healthy" (p. 20). When have you experienced a time when fear helped or protected you?
5. In chapter 2, Amy suggests that "worry is fashionable" and that we use it to prove we are in demand and responsible. How do you see this appearance issue manifest in your own life or those around you?
6. Amy mentions the idea of "sabbath rest" when she tells the story of the wandering Israelites and God's gift of manna (pp. 77-78). How does practicing sabbath rest show faith in God's provision?
7. Chapter 4 says that our worry offends God (p. 80). How does this statement impact your conception of God's personality?
8. How difficult might it have been for the Israelites to place their faith in God compared to people living now (p. 107)?
9. Do you agree with the cognitive-behavioral view that thoughts and beliefs are responsible for behaviors and feelings (pp. 111-112)? Reflect on the noted Bible passages when explaining your view.
10. Does the knowledge that our brains physically change in response to anxiety (or lack thereof) excite you or scare you (p. 115)?
11. Read James 4:13-16 on pages 140-41. Where do you draw the line between responsible preparation and making plans that ignore God's authority over your life?
12. As mentioned in chapter 8, how should the idea of being a caretaker, not an owner, impact your feelings of responsibility and stress?
13. How should focusing on who God is change our mindset regarding worry?

A Conversation with . . . **Amy Simpson**

What drove you to write this book? Doesn't writing about all the stressors we have in this world just make us have more anxiety?

Amy Simpson: God began to open my eyes to the habit of worry—and just how much it controlled me—through a series of challenging circumstances. My husband and I were dealing with some serious financial stress and at the same time felt strongly, over a period of time, that I should resign my position as a publishing executive and devote a substantial portion of my time to writing. Clearly, it made no sense for us to make a risky change in my employment status. But no matter how many times we told ourselves that, this sense of calling did not go away.

As I was wrestling through the "what ifs" and the fears that were keeping me from obeying God, I kept asking God for reassurance, something that would give me a sense that everything would be okay. But instead of changing our circumstances, and instead of giving me the concrete answers I was looking for—what I was really longing for was a peek at the future—he just taught me more about himself. I saw how my "what ifs" reveal my appalling lack of trust not only that God will take care of me, but that God's plans are better than mine, even if my worst fears are realized.

Interestingly, I think writing the book helped me become a less anxious person. I was able to sit and really think about some of the things that worry me and realize that when they're put in perspective, they're not as big as they seem. And I realized that I often worry about other things only because someone is actively encouraging me to feel worried about them, not because they're important to me or because worrying will help at all.

Did the process of writing *Troubled Minds* influence *Anxious*?

Amy: On the surface, I think *Troubled Minds* helped me learn some things that I used in writing *Anxious*; for example, what anxiety disorders are and thinking about the distinctions between anxiety, fear and worry. I think *Troubled Minds* also helped me write with more sensitivity toward people who do have anxiety disorders. But on a deeper level, the experience of writing *Troubled Minds* was one big act of faith and courage, so I was working out some of the themes of *Anxious* in my own life and spirit as I wrote

Troubled Minds. I wrote *Troubled Minds* right after I left my executive position, and I was going through the related major life transition and dealing with all the uncertainties that came with it.

You write that this book is not meant to shame people who have anxiety disorders. Why is that distinction important?

Amy: It's important because I don't want people with anxiety disorders, and people who struggle to get their anxiety under control, to feel judged or condemned by what I've written. I've spent a lot of time, words and emotional energy trying to fight the stigma attached to mental illness, particularly in the church. Anxiety disorders are often misunderstood as just "excessive worry," as if people are choosing to indulge the habit of worry more than they should and the solution is to just stop it. For people with anxiety disorders, worry may not be any more habitual than it is for their next-door neighbors; their bodies and minds may be simply unable to turn off that anxious response that God built into us as a gift to keep us safe. There's no reason to feel ashamed of a runaway biological process like that. The solution is in retraining the brain to respond in a healthier way to stimuli, often through therapy, and for many people in taking medication at least for the short term. I've written *Anxious* for people who have a choice, as most of us do, and who choose to respond to fear with worry—as most of us do.

How do you battle worry on a daily basis?

Amy: The experiences of seeing how prevalent worry is in my life, then writing about it, have made me very conscious of this ongoing battle. Sometimes I try to address worry by doing something: relaxing, taking a break, praying, exercising, talking to a friend. But as I wrote about in *Anxious*, and as Jesus taught when he was on earth, our behavior reflects what we have in our hearts and minds. The key to real behavior change is change in the way we think. So when I find myself worrying, I try to shift my focus and reorient myself around what I believe is true about God. I check my attitude toward the future: Am I trying to see something I don't have the ability to see? I check my attitude toward possessions and people: Am I trying to hang onto something that really isn't mine? I try to pull back to a bigger-picture perspective: How important is this really? Am I focused on what matters to God in this situation? These changes in thinking can cause changes in my behavior and can help me to stop worrying.

THE ATTENTIVE LIFE

Discerning God's Presence in All Things

Leighton Ford

If you're busy, distracted, rushing through each day, you might be feeling disconnected from God, unable to see how he's working. You might be missing him. But the way toward him starts with a pause and a prayer—with intention and attention—and becomes a way of life, awake and alive to the peaceful, powerful presence of God. Using the rich monastic tradition of praying the hours, Leighton Ford will walk with you, helping you pay attention to God's work in you and around you throughout each day and in different seasons of your life.

"I thank God for The Attentive Life. *It provides an antidote to the primary spiritual problem of our day: distraction.* The Attentive Life *is the mature reflections of one who has spent a lifetime walking in the way of Jesus."*

Richard J. Foster, author of *Celebration of Discipline*

"Drawing on the wisdom of many traditions, The Attentive Life *is a warm invitation to wake up, not just to the reality of God but to what is deepest inside of us. This is a gold mine of wisdom and balance, a challenging thought on every page."*

Ronald Rolheiser, author of *The Holy Longing*

ABOUT THE AUTHOR: Leighton Ford is president of Leighton Ford Ministries, which seeks to empower young Christian leaders. He has communicated Christ to millions of people around the globe, serving for thirty years with the Billy Graham Evangelistic Association, as chairman of the Lausanne Committee for World Evangelization and as a board member for World Vision. *Time* magazine has singled him out as being "among the most influential preachers of an active gospel."

◆ QUESTIONS

1. Leighton Ford looks to attentiveness as a way "to deepen my own friendship with God and to walk with others who want to do the same" (p. 10). Do you have a similar or different purpose for learning to live an attentive life?
2. On pages 37-39 Leighton lists the qualities of attentiveness. Which ones are most difficult for you to develop? Which ones come naturally?
3. "Attentiveness is a learned practice; so is inattentiveness" (p. 67). Are there examples you can cite from your own life or society that encourage inattentiveness?
4. Prime is "the hour of the deliberate beginning of the day," or the time we start doing each day (p. 81). What is your "prime" time and your attitude toward what you'll be doing?
5. Leighton chooses three words to sum up the concept of prime: abiding, indwelling and contemplation. Which word or concept have you discovered helps you to be more attentive in everyday life?
6. Jason Read's story demonstrates how apathy, indifference or an "I don't care" attitude can enter into life (pp. 120-21). Where do you see this attitude in society as a whole? Where do you see it in your own life?
7. Leighton writes that sin—the wrong-centeredness of who we are —is the root cause of our inattention (p. 124). Why do you think it is so hard for us to be God-focused instead of self-focused?
8. Chapter 7 talks about the dark times of life. Looking at the list of five steps on page 148, which will bring you into greater communion with God? Which is most challenging to do during the dark times?
9. "I know how to be busy and to move purposefully. Do I also know how to stop?" (p. 176). How do you respond to Leighton's question? When are the times that you stop without feeling guilty?
10. The book is organized by the "hours" of our lives. How has looking at your life through different "hours" helped you be more attentive during your day and the stage of life you are at today?
11. Included at the end of each chapter is a "Practicing Attentiveness" section. Which of these practices was most helpful to encourage attentiveness?

BALANCED CHRISTIANITY

Expanded Edition

John Stott

Christians tend to polarize. Some have an intellectual faith, while others are more emotional. Some focus on structure, while others focus on freedom. And some champion evangelism, while others advocate for social action. John Stott's classic statement of balanced Christianity shows how we can hold these tensions together in biblical, faithful ways.

"'Balance' for John Stott is not about a neutral middle. Instead, it is the vigorous act of faithful both/and living—frequently holding to two extremes rather than sliding to one or the other. . . . Though first written for a different time, his words are still poignant and provocative."

Mark Labberton, author of *Called*

"In this book John Stott first opened my mind to the delightful joy of truths we cannot always resolve but to which we can commit ourselves in tension. . . . In your hands is one of the great tracts of twentieth-century evangelicalism. Savor it."

Scot McKnight, Northern Seminary

ABOUT THE AUTHOR: John R. W. Stott (1921–2011) has been known worldwide as a preacher, evangelist and communicator of Scripture. A leader among evangelicals in Britain, the United States and around the world, Stott was a principal framer of the landmark Lausanne Covenant (1974). His many books have sold millions of copies around the world and in dozens of languages. Stott was honored by *Time* magazine in 2005 as one of the 100 Most Influential People in the World and was named in the Queen's New Year Honours List 2005 as Commander of the Order of the British Empire.

◆ QUESTIONS

1. From the title, what does the word *balanced* mean to John Stott? Was this your understanding prior to reading this book? If not, how was it different?
2. How can we actually practice "holding to two extremes rather than sliding to one or the other" (p. 1)?
3. Stott identifies a great tragedy of Christianity as polarization (p. 7). Since this first edition was written in 1975, the topics causing polarization at Stott's time are likely different than today. What do you think were the polarizing topics then? How have they been resolved or do they continue?
4. What topics cause polarization in evangelical Christians today?
5. Stott lists our areas of unity (pp. 7-8). Why do you think this does not prevent us from polarization?
6. Do you agree with Stott that "we should not try to press our position . . . on other Christian consciences" (pp. 8-9). Why or why not?
7. Stott quotes Charles Simeon: "The truth is not in the middle, and not in one extreme, but in both extremes" (p. 11). Can you explain this?
8. Reread the example on page 37 about gadflies and watchdogs. How are we, the church, doing in living up to Stott's challenge?
9. Stott noticed a widespread quest for the free, the flexible, the spontaneous and the unstructured (p. 40). What do you see in the church today as a result of this debate of the past? Is it still an issue today?
10. Generally social justice efforts are welcomed in the church today. Does it surprise you that this wasn't always the norm? How can understanding this change in application of the Christian faith help us live a balanced Christianity?
11. In the interview Stott says Christians ought to be optimists but not utopians. Which are you? Do you agree that faith and pessimism don't go together?
12. Many of the examples in this book are now part of history. Was it helpful to see how many of these debates have played out and shaped the church today?

An Interview with . . . *John Stott (1995)*

Your ministry now stretches back over fifty years. How have you changed over that time, both as a person and as a minister?

John Stott: I'm afraid I was very naive when I was ordained. I was very much an activist more than a thinker. I saw needs and wanted immediately to meet them, and this crowded out my studies, really.

Don't some people fear that a renewed emphasis on social concern might muffle the call to evangelism?

Stott: I've really no wish for missionaries to change their role. I think there is a real need for evangelists who are not engaged in holistic mission because their calling is evangelism.

It seems to me that evangelicalism has fragmented into different groups, with different heroes, different events, different publishers, different cultures. How should we think of ourselves now?

Stott: I don't mind plurality as long as it goes hand-in-hand with unity—but I suppose you could say I've given a great deal of my life to the preservation and development of the unity of the evangelical constituency, because it has been a great concern of mine.

What are the current causes of our fragmentation?

Stott: Well, we fragment over what we regard as issues of principle—but often the real reason is personal, isn't it? When we're afraid, we withdraw into our own fellowships and ghettos where we feel secure with like-minded people. I'm aware of that fear in myself; it's part of our basic human insecurity. We're looking for contexts in which we can be supported rather than questioned.

Does it alarm you to hear people calling themselves "post-evangelical"?

Stott: Yes. I don't know what they mean, but it does alarm me. If you are "post" anything, you are leaving something behind, and I want to know what it is. If it's our many faults and failures, fine—but that's not post-evangelicalism, it's post-twisted-evangelicalism.

What are the weaknesses of evangelicalism?

Stott: We've discussed our rugged individualism and the difficulty we have in cooperating with one another. Another, I think, is our dogmatism. Instead of remembering Deuteronomy 29:29, we are dogmatic about even the things which God has kept secret. We're often not prepared to admit a certain agnosticism, which is a very evangelical thing, if we are alluding to what God has not revealed. We have many weaknesses.

Some people might say that the church is simply very conservative. It only joins . . . movements for change under pressure from secular forces in society.

Stott: I wish it were always Christians who took the initiative in seeking needed social change—but I am still thankful when others take the initiative and Christians follow, even under secular pressure. We must not set secular fashion and the Holy Spirit over against each other, as being always and inevitably incompatible. Public opinion isn't always wrong. What is wrong is to bow down before it uncritically, like reeds shaken by the wind.

What is the theological basis for Christian involvement today? Is it enough to speak of "salt and light"?

Stott: There is the nature of God himself. God is interested in and concerned about more than religion: he is the God of creation as well as of the covenant. He is the lover of justice: this is his nature. He is the kind of God who protects and champions the oppressed. And if that is the kind of God he is, then clearly his people have got to be the same.

Are we too ready in the West to accept the view that a successful church is also an affluent one?

Stott: I suppose it is because some people see prosperity as a mark of God's blessing, even today, that they can't come to terms with poverty. I think we have to have the courage to reject the health-and-wealth gospel absolutely. It's a false gospel.

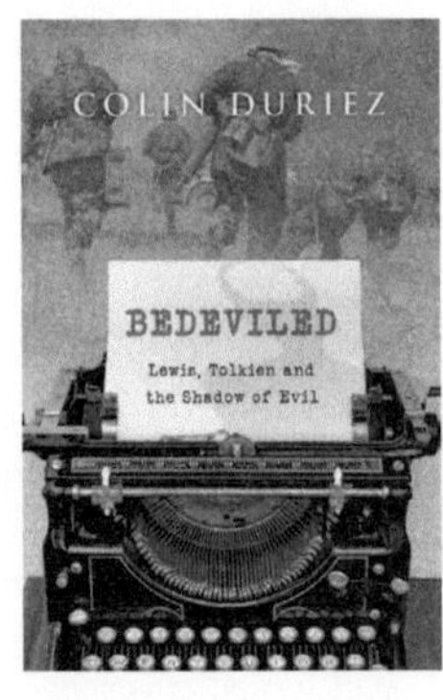

BEDEVILED

Lewis, Tolkien and the Shadow of Evil

Colin Duriez

The battle between good and evil—in both the seen and unseen worlds—was as clearly at play in the era of C. S. Lewis and his friends in the Oxford literary group, the Inklings, as in our own era.

Among the Inklings, Lewis was at the forefront of writing on human pain, suffering, devilry, miracles and the supernatural, with books like *The Screwtape Letters* and more. J. R. R. Tolkien's *The Lord of the Rings* trilogy offers another rich resource with much to say to the World War II era and beyond. Delving into the interplay between good and evil, these pages enlighten us to the way of goodness and the promise of a far country as we explore the way out of the shadow of evil.

"This important book celebrates strong hope over and against the dire forces of darkness that beset us. Together, Lewis, Tolkien and Duriez raise the victory flag with high courage, wisdom and joy."

Monika B. Hilder, Trinity Western University

"Nobody knows more about the respective canons of C. S. Lewis and J. R. R. Tolkien or their collaborative friendship than Colin Duriez."

Bruce L. Edwards, editor of *C. S. Lewis: Life, Works, Legacy*

ABOUT THE AUTHOR: Colin Duriez has taught, written and spoken worldwide on C. S. Lewis, J. R. R. Tolkien and the Inklings for nearly thirty years. He has appeared as a commentator on the extended-version film DVDs of *The Lord of the Rings* trilogy (Peter Jackson, director), PBS's *The Question of God,* which compared C. S. Lewis and Sigmund Freud, and the Sony DVD *Ringers* about Tolkien fandom and the impact of Tolkien on popular culture.

◆ QUESTIONS

1. How do you think the writings of Lewis and Tolkien would have been different if World War II had not been happening in their own country?
2. Do you think Lewis's writings would have been as successful had he not found faith in God? Do you think he would have written at all?
3. Beyond *The Screwtape Letters,* can you name any other writings from Lewis, Tolkien or the Inklings that had a Hitler-like character?
4. Do you think in writing *The Lord of the Rings* and The Chronicles of Narnia series Tolkien and Lewis wanted to change things in the world? Or was it a way to process the evil in the world around them?
5. Think a bit about the friendship between Lewis and Tolkien. Can you think of any other literary partnerships like theirs?
6. Duriez writes in chapter 1, "Noticeable is Tolkien and Lewis's perception of a devilish plot against humanity with the machine and applied science as the modern form of magic." Do you think these two hated technology and thought it evil? Where else is this theme prevalent in writings from the mid-twentieth century?
7. Think about the symbolism behind the ring in *The Lord of the Rings*. How does it demonstrate evil and devilry? Can you think of any other books that use a similar motif?
8. If you could sit down with any of the Inklings and have an hour-long conversation, who would you pick and why?
9. Why do you think Tolkien "did not approve of his friend C. S. Lewis writing theology for the general public," as he did in The Chronicles of Narnia series?
10. What do you think Lewis meant when he wrote "any amount of theology can now be smuggled into people's minds under the cover of romance without their knowing it" (chap. 5)?
11. Think about Lewis's upbringing as described in the early chapters. How do you think that influenced his later writing?
12. Lewis and Tolkien both viewed good and evil as very black and white. Do you think there is more gray area today?

BOTH-AND

Living the Christ-Centered Life in an Either-Or World

Rich Nathan with Insoo Kim

It's an Either-Or world. We find ourselves caught between competing factions, secular or religious, conservative or liberal. But the Christian faith holds together seemingly contradictory ideas: Jesus is both human and divine; God is both three and one. There is a paradoxical power in the both-and.

Rich Nathan and Insoo Kim show how Christians can live out the fullness of the gospel through the both-and. The answer is not to choose one or the other, but to hold both together for a richer, more holistic experience of Christianity. Then we will live into the realities of the kingdom of God, both now and not yet, on earth as it is in heaven.

"Too many of us have a gospel with a hole in it, or as pastors Rich Nathan and Insoo Kim write, we have an 'either-or' gospel. . . . Be warned: following their wisdom will turn you into a radical disciple of Jesus Christ!"

Richard Stearns, president of World Vision US

"Both-And *is a prophetic word for our day. It is relevant. It is challenging. It is compassionate. It is courageous."*

Richard J. Foster, author of *Celebration of Discipline* and *Sanctuary of the Soul*

ABOUT THE AUTHORS: Rich Nathan is senior pastor of Vineyard Columbus and a popular international conference speaker. He has served on the Vineyard's national board for nearly two decades and is currently serving as the Large Church Task Force leader for the Vineyard.

Insoo Kim serves as the pastor of ministry strategies at Vineyard Columbus. He is also the director of the Church Planting Residency Program, which exists to launch new church plants from Vineyard Columbus. Insoo is also a regular preacher at weekend services.

◆ QUESTIONS

1. What do the authors mean by "both-and"?
2. What prevents Christians from living in the "both-and" tension?
3. Throughout the book, the authors describe several extremes within Christianity. Which of these challenged or convicted you? Or are the authors creating false polarizations?
4. The authors list three obstacles that keep us from praying for healing: we have a limited worldview, we give up too soon and we want to look good (pp. 180-183). How have any of these prevented you from praying for something?
5. The authors write, "In contemporary Christianity, we have almost entirely lost the view that the kingdom of God is not yet fully here. Almost no Christians I know . . . think much about eternity or talk much about our future hope" (p. 200). Have you found this to be the case? If so, why might this be?
6. The authors observe that some subjects seem to be disregarded, demeaned or closed for discussion within the church (p. 14). Has this been your experience? What was the subject?
7. In what contexts does the "both-and" method not apply?
8. The authors differentiate between dogma, doctrines and opinions and claim that "most of us Christians spend our time fighting with each other about . . . opinions" (pp. 226-228). Are there any questions of opinion so vital that they are worth the divisions they cause?
9. The authors take clear positions on several controversial issues. Did their views of charismatic theology, immigration, church and state relations, same-sex marriage or gender roles in the church affect your reading of the book's central argument?
10. Can you think of more "both-and" tensions other than those mentioned?
11. For each of the chapter pairs addressed in this book, where do you think most Christians fall on the following scale? Do you agree with the authors that we should strive to be on the far right?
    Either-Or -- Both-And
12. What good could come from taking up the "both-and" approach? Where could it potentially go wrong?

BROKE

What Financial Desperation Revealed about God's Abundance

Caryn Rivadeneira

"*Broke* was not in the cards for me. . . . Girls—then women—like us stay strong through it all. A little (or big) financial setback doesn't break us. Or our connection to God."

In the midst of a financial and spiritual desert, Caryn questioned God's goodness, wondering how he could feel so far away. Doesn't God promise blessing to those who serve him? Doesn't he hear his faithful followers' cries for provision and help? Join in Caryn's journey as she pursues God even when bruised, battered and broken by life. You'll laugh and cry with her as she experiences spiritual blessing and discovers God's goodness in ways she never expected.

"If you like your Jesus sugary sweet, don't read Broke. *If you don't think irreverent humor is next to godliness, don't read* Broke. . . . *But if you like gritty and funny, honest and faithful, go for* Broke.*"*

Karen Swallow Prior, author of *Booked: Literature in the Soul of Me*

"Rivadeneira reminds us that the abundant life is quite a ride, and that our ticket has been paid in full. All we have to pay is our attention."

Carolyn Weber, author of *Holy Is the Day*

ABOUT THE AUTHOR: Caryn Rivadeneira is a writer, speaker and regular contributor at the *Her.menutics* blog. At Moody Radio she works on air and as a producer for *Midday Connection.* She spent years as an editor at Christianity Today's magazines and currently serves on the worship staff at Elmhurst Christian Reformed Church. She is a member of Ink Creative Collective, a community of Christian women writers and speakers.

◆ QUESTIONS

1. *Broke* is a book about money—that's not really about money. Spiritually speaking how can we be broken?
2. On page 19, Caryn writes, "Realizing God heard me kicked off a lifelong journey of following a God who I understood wanted a relationship with me." What does being heard mean to you?
3. Caryn refers to "the God who sometimes takes away so that we can see more clearly" (p. 25). How did Caryn experience this? Have you had a similar experience that helped you know him more?
4. "My life of abundance had no room for understanding what praying for daily bread meant" (p. 28). Can you relate to this statement? Why or why not?
5. Caryn seems to take a lot of liberties in her prayer with God. What do you make of the tone in this prayer, "You've really got to do better on this other stuff. You've really got to pony up" (p. 30)? Have you prayed like this? Would you? Why or why not?
6. A love of mysteries and exploring drove Caryn to look for signs of God. How has your curiosity shaped your faith, your Bible reading, your church-going?
7. Caryn jokes about once believing she could be so "helpful to God and his kingdom" (p. 53). When have you felt like your gifts were indispensible to God?
8. Caryn feels confident in hearing God's actual voice at times. How does this strike you? Real? Way out there? Do you believe God still speaks in actual words? How have you heard God?
9. Caryn writes that God uses coincidences to make himself known. What are some of the ways you've experienced God's grand coincidences in your life?
10. Caryn defines prayer as a conversation with God in which we imagine him there (p. 113). How might this definition affect your own prayer life?
11. Where did your "wild-and-wooly, twist-turny faith journey" begin (p. 132)? If those words don't apply to your story, what words would you use to describe it? What have you discovered?

An Excerpt from . . . **Broke**

Last summer—on the first coolish, crispish summer morning after a week of scorching 100-degree days—I took my Bible and copy of *Jesus Calling* out to my back deck. I laughed when I noticed the steam rising up from my cup of coffee. The nice, Christian lady out doing her "quiet time" on the back deck as the sun rose (albeit, on the *other* side of the house): such a stereotype. But one I'd certainly never nailed before.

If Chaos is my muse and my muse is really the Holy Spirit, it makes sense that God and I often find each other and speak to each other best as I retreat into my mind in the middle of noise. Though silence and solitude are tried and true spiritual practices, I fail at them constantly. Mostly because, in silence and calm and peace and quiet, my soul and mind get restless. And true to form, as I sat like the Good Christian Lady on my back deck with my steaming coffee, almost right away I noticed the "teenage" bunny and mentally remarked how big he'd gotten. I wondered if I could go cut the tops off some strawberries. *If I toss some into that weed patch, will he find them? Will he eat them? Or will my human scent drive him away?*

And then the neighbor's car beeped twice. Doors unlocked, an alarm shut off from the remote. Huh? The neighbor normally doesn't leave for work this early. But then I noticed their son—the *human* teenager. *Ah, yes. Up for baseball. Makes sense.*

And while God is indeed the God of all these things, my mind had not exactly stayed focused on him. Hence my trouble with "quiet time" and this particular discipline.

So I kicked back in my deck chair and looked across the potted mint plants to the white loveseat against the deck rail. The image started fuzzy but sharpened as the coffee kicked in. I imagined Jesus sitting there—cross-legged, adjusting the ever-slipping red cushions. He had khaki shorts on—a bit ragged around the edges—and a tan *ThinkChristian* T-shirt. I got mine because I'm a regular contributor to the site, but I wondered how he got his. Didn't matter—what an endorsement! Jesus wearing your T-shirt? *I'll have to tell Josh* (the editor), I thought.

Already, my focus on Jesus was slipping, so I just started talking.

"So Jesus," I said, "you really are more present in these early, backyard quiet times I'm always reading about."

I smiled. He smiled back.

"Not more," Jesus said, through my mouth. "Just always."

I sighed, pulling a face. Might as well get truthful, to the point here. I never know when a child will wake and come yelling for me.

"I'm getting a little tired of the waiting, you know."

"I know."

"Can you give me a clue? A little hint as to how much longer?"

"Soon," he said.

"And very soon?" I smile again. Jesus laughed. He knows how I love the old spirituals.

"But Jesus, really? We're getting kind of desperate here. We've taken huge steps and big leaps of faith—in obedience. We're trying to follow you, and you're still sort of leaving us hanging."

"Not hanging. You just don't see."

"Right," I said. "You know the plans you have for us, yada, yada, yada."

"Yes," he says. "And they are not plans to harm you. As you know."

"It sure doesn't feel that way. It feels like you brought us into this desert to die."

"No. I go ahead of you," Jesus said, "I'm knocking down mountains and leveling roads for you. This desert is going to blossom. Remember, I've called you by name. You are mine. I've got you."

CALLED

The Crisis and Promise of Following Jesus Today

Mark Labberton

The most urgent call upon God's people is to live as followers of Jesus. The most indicting critique against the church is as simple: its failure to do so.

We long to renew our hope for a world broken and hurting. And it is we, God's people living in the power of the Holy Spirit, who are called to become this hope and flourish while in exile. Here is the crisis: we are made and redeemed for this calling, but it slides through our fingers. Here is the promise: living and practicing who and why we are is our Christian vocation whenever and wherever we may be. Will you answer the call?

"When I read Mark Labberton's writing I can almost hear Jesus say, 'Well, there it is. That's what I was literally dying to tell you.'"

M. Craig Barnes, president, Princeton Seminary

"Called *is a book that will call to you with a vision for a life well lived in God's presence in the world that God loves."*

Ruth Haley Barton, author of *Sacred Rhythms*

ABOUT THE AUTHOR: Mark Labberton is president of Fuller Theological Seminary in Pasadena, California. He came to Fuller after sixteen years as senior pastor of First Presbyterian Church of Berkeley, California. He contributes to the mission of the global church as a senior fellow of International Justice Mission and he is the author of *The Dangerous Act of Loving Your Neighbor* and *The Dangerous Act of Worship*.

This title is also available as an audiobook from ivpress.com/audio.

◆ QUESTIONS

1. The subtitle of the book is "the crisis and promise of following Jesus today." How did you understand what the author, Mark Labberton, meant by this prior to completing the book?
2. Mark expresses understanding as to why "the lives of Christians seem too constricted to have any relevance to the real world" (pp. 5-6). Do you think this is a common perception? Why or why not?
3. An orchestra is given as an example of human flourishing, "which is always about the one and the many" (p. 12). Where have you witnessed or experienced human flourishing?
4. Call is described as "God's desire for all of our lives as ambassadors of God's kingdom. This is our primary call. This primary call for *all* of us leads naturally and secondarily to God's call for *each* of us" (p. 17). How does this distinction help you? Or not? In your experience has one "call" been emphasized over the other?
5. In chapter 2, descriptive labels are given to the church (pp. 28-31) and the world (pp. 32-37). Which ring most true of the church and your experience in the world?
6. Mark says "We must face up to the enormous loss of credibility between the faith the church professes and the actions we demonstrate. Nothing else should matter to the church of Jesus Christ as much as this" (p. 38). Do you agree or disagree with the author's diagnosis of the church and emphasis on correcting it?
7. The author writes that suffering may be a sign that Christians today live in exile, not the promised land. Is this idea new to you? Do you agree?
8. The author says the concept of the "promised land" and the "American Dream" have affected our churches. What similarities do you see?
9. Belief is very important in Christianity. How do you respond to the author's distinctions in chapter 5 between believing in Jesus and following Jesus?
10. A repeated statement throughout the book is that our call is to follow Jesus in all we do. How has this concept affected your understanding of calling?

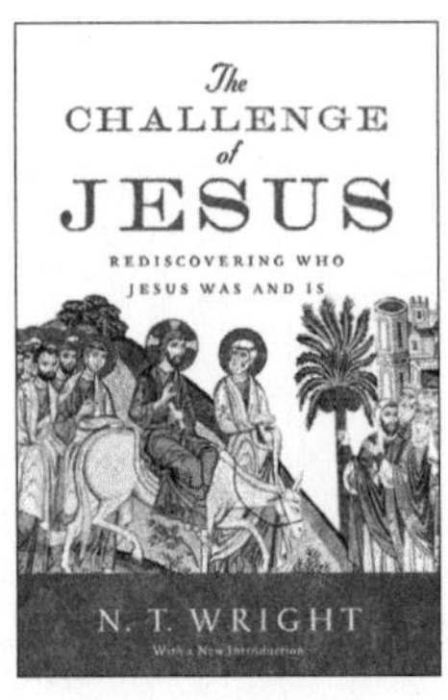

THE CHALLENGE OF JESUS

Rediscovering Who Jesus Was and Is

N. T. Wright

Out of his own commitment to both historical scholarship and Christian ministry, N. T. Wright challenges us to roll up our sleeves and take seriously the study of the historical Jesus. He writes, "We cannot assume that by saying the word *Jesus,* still less the word *Christ,* we are automatically in touch with the real Jesus who walked and talked in first-century Palestine. . . . Only by hard, historical work can we move toward a fuller comprehension of what the Gospels themselves were trying to say."

The Challenge of Jesus poses a double-edged challenge: to grow in our understanding of the historical Jesus within the Palestinian world of the first century, and to follow Jesus more faithfully into the postmodern world of the twenty-first century.

"A refreshing and inspiring read for those who take both conservative faith and historical scholarship seriously."

***Library Journal,* January 2000**

ABOUT THE AUTHOR: N. T. Wright has written over thirty books, including *Simply Christian, The Original Jesus, What Saint Paul Really Said, Jesus and the Victory of God* and *The Meaning of Jesus.* His N. T. Wright For Everyone Series includes commentaries covering the entire New Testament.

Formerly bishop of Durham in England, Wright has taught at leading institutions all over the world. A sought-after commentator, Wright writes frequently for newspapers in England and has been interviewed by radio and television broadcasters including ABC, NBC, CNN, PBS and NPR.

◆ QUESTIONS

1. Wright says that Christianity necessarily entails "doing business with history." Do you agree or disagree?

2. How might sloppy thinking about the real historical Jesus distort our praying and discipleship (p. 10)?

3. What is the "theological exile" that many first century Jews believed they were living in (p. 36)? Why is this significant?

4. Wright states that the clash between Jesus and the Pharisees was not that they believed in justification by works but that they believed Israel needed to leave off her "frantic and paranoid self-defense" (p. 58). Do you agree or disagree?

5. What are some events in the life of Jesus that show that he understood himself to be the Messiah (p. 81)?

6. How is the God of the Bible different than the god of Enlightenment Deism? Have you noticed deistic tendencies in your own view of God (p. 96)?

7. Do you agree with Wright that the nature of Jesus' knowledge of his divinity was something like an "awareness of vocation" (p. 122)?

8. Why do you think alternative portrayals of Jesus are so prevalent in our culture? Why do you think so many people seem skeptical of the earliest historical accounts of Jesus and are easily persuaded by alternatives (p. 128)?

9. A crucified would-be messiah was nothing new in the first century. Imagine you are a first century Jew and your messiah was crucified. What would you think and feel (pp. 138-139)?

10. Wright says, "The whole point of New Testament Christianity is that the End came forward into the present in Jesus the Messiah." What does this mean? Is this understanding of Christianity new to you (p. 178)?

11. Wright says that the key for translating Jesus' message to our contemporaries is that we are made in the image of God. What does he mean when he says the image of God is "not just a fact, it is vocation"? Have you heard the image of God discussed this way before (p. 183)?

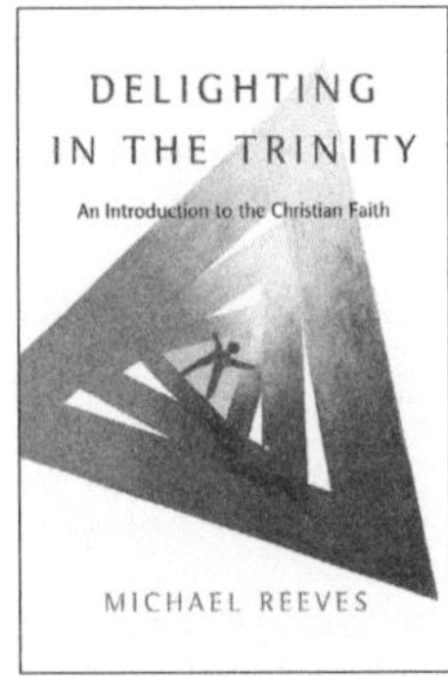

DELIGHTING IN THE TRINITY

An Introduction to the Christian Faith

Michael Reeves

Why is God love? Because God is a Trinity. Why can we be saved? Because God is a Trinity. How are we able to live the Christian life? Through the Trinity.

In this lively book, we find an introduction to Christianity and the Christian life that is from start to finish rooted in our triune God—Father, Son and Spirit. Not only do we understand the person and work of Christ through the Trinity, but also prayer, the church and every aspect of our faith. With wit and clarity, Reeves draws from church history down to the present referencing a wide range of notable teachers and preachers. Here is a rich and enjoyable portrayal of the basic beliefs of Christianity that opens up the profound and life-changing truths of our faith.

"If your life as a Christian has become at all routine or you simply wish to be freshly amazed at the transformative love of the Trinity for you, read Delighting in the Trinity.*"*

Dan Cruver, author of *Reclaiming Adoption*

"Convinced that 'the triunity of God is the secret of his beauty,' Reeves writes from a full heart, with contagious enthusiasm for the Trinity."

Fred Sanders, Biola University

ABOUT THE AUTHOR: Michael Reeves (PhD, King's College) is an author, theologian, historian and professor who teaches at Wales Evangelical School of Theology (WEST) and is the director of Union, a WEST initiative that puts the theological academy back in the local church context. He was associate minister at All Souls Church, Langham Place and is the author of books such as *The Unquenchable Flame, Discovering the Heart of the Reformation, On Giants' Shoulders* and *The Good God.*

◆ QUESTIONS

1. Reeves writes, "Neither a problem nor a technicality, the triune being of God is the vital oxygen of Christian life and joy" (p. 18). Do you resonate with this assessment? Why or why not?
2. When trying to describe God, why is it important to start with the Son?
3. How does God as described in Christianity differ from the gods in other religions?
4. What roles do the Father, Son, and Holy Spirit play in creation? How does this affect your understanding of what it means to be made in the image of God?
5. Through the work of Jesus, God has made us his children. Do you feel you have embraced your identity as a child of God? What does that look like?
6. Does defining sin as misdirected love seem accurate to you? Why or why not?
7. What are your expectations when you read the Bible? What can be gained from asking "What do I learn here of Christ?" rather than "What does this mean for me, right now?"
8. What does the Holy Spirit make possible for us?
9. How does our delight in Christ—or lack thereof—relate to evangelism?
10. Do you find Reeves's description of holiness compelling? Why or why not?
11. How might you explain God's wrath in the context of God's love?
12. What would you say the Christian life is about? How has this book affected your answer?

DWELL

Life with God for the World

Barry D. Jones
Foreword by Michael Frost

Popular notions of Christian spirituality today tend to focus on getting us out of the world or getting the world out of us. But Jesus offers a radical model for living. As the Incarnate One who dwelt among us, he teaches us how to dwell *in* the world for the sake *of* the world.

What does a Christian life deeply rooted in the logic of the incarnation look like? Missional teacher and pastor Barry Jones shares his vision for authentic Christian spirituality focused on becoming more like Jesus. We dwell in a specific place and time in history, with unique bodies and in a world for which God has great purposes of redemption. This presence in the world should lead us to pattern our lives after the life of Jesus who was a boundary breaker, a shalom-maker, a people-keeper and a wounded-healer.

"Barry Jones offers an assessment of our broken world and the common errors and bent practices that subvert a rich engagement. Then he shows us the horizon: a vision of the coming shalom of God's kingdom."

Len Hjalmarson, author of *Missional Spirituality*

ABOUT THE AUTHOR: Barry D. Jones (PhD, Wheaton College) serves as associate professor of pastoral ministries and spiritual formation at Dallas Theological Seminary. With an acute desire to train future leaders who are deeply rooted in their faith and vitally engaged in the world, Barry has served in a variety of ministry capacities including as a youth pastor, a camp and retreat speaker, and currently as a teaching pastor at Irving Bible Church.

◆ QUESTIONS

1. The introduction establishes "missional spirituality" by explaining the potential pathologies associated with both spirituality (Narcissus) and missionality (Prometheus). How do the two compare?
2. How does living into God's story instead of *living up* to Christian spirituality (chap. 1) free you as you navigate your own story?
3. Barry notes, "Sometimes knowing the end of the story from the beginning provides a depth of meaning and understanding you might not grasp otherwise" (p. 35). Does knowing the "end of the story" in your Christian walk inform and transform the way you live now? How?
4. How do you respond to the "vandalism of shalom" in the world? Does sacred discontentment (pp. 64-65) fuel your responsibility and the way you respond?
5. Discuss the three things the Spirit has come to do (pp. 74-79)? Have you seen the Holy Spirit in any of these roles within your own life?
6. What's the significance behind Barry proposing we ask people if they have a communal relationship with Jesus versus a personal relationship (p. 81)? Do you think he's on to something?
7. How are these words—*attentiveness, receptivity, embodiment, community, rhythm*—also ways in which men and women in the church have engaged with God, ways of "countercultural grammar"?
8. What four things does Barry contend worship is designed to accomplish? What is going on in worship that leads to these four elements?
9. Can you empathize with Barry's experience of "sabbath keeping" found in chapter 8? Does the uncovering of the sabbath as a chance to be fully alive rather than dying to self appeal to you?
10. Barry offers practical ways we can pursue connections and practice the discipline of hospitality (p. 207). Which one can you commit to today to help others "taste and see" the beauty of Christian community?
11. Having looked at the "logic of the incarnation" in the way it informs our vision for spiritual life, how can you create a space for God's vision?
12. How has *Dwell* helped you understand the balance of inward and outward, advance and retreat, and formation and mission with respect to your discipleship journey?

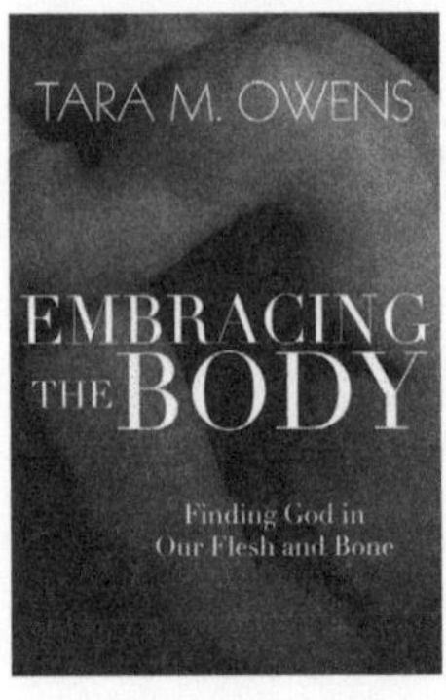

EMBRACING THE BODY

Finding God in Our Flesh and Bone

Tara M. Owens

Our bodies teach us about God, and God communicates to us through our bodies. Our bodies are more *good* than we can possibly imagine them to be. Yet at times we may struggle with feelings of shame and guilt or even pride in regard to our bodies. What is God trying to do through our skin and bones?

Spiritual director Tara Owens invites you to listen to your thoughts about your body in a way that draws you closer to God, calling you to explore how your spirituality is intimately tied to your physicality. She guides you to see your body not as an inconvenience but as a place where you can meet the holy in a new way—a place to embrace God's glorious intention.

"This book is beautiful, learned and wise. It will make you think, and it will make you want to say 'amen'—and, more important, it will enable you more fully to live as a body."

Lauren F. Winner, author of *Girl Meets God* and *Still*

"Truth. Beauty. Revelation. Those are just some of the words to describe Embracing the Body.*"*

Stasi Eldredge, coauthor of *Captivating*

ABOUT THE AUTHOR: Tara M. Owens is a Certified Spiritual Director and the senior editor for *Conversations Journal.* Owens also provides spiritual direction through her ministry Anam Cara and is a part-time instructor for the Benedictine Spiritual Formation Program at Benet Hill Monastery, both based in Colorado Springs.

◆ QUESTIONS

1. The author says that the body of Christ as a whole needs you to have a holistic, healthy relationship with your own body in order for it to function as it was designed. Do you agree with this? Why or why not?
2. Chapter 1 tells a story of being warned against invisible trains as a way of keeping her out of danger. In what ways have you seen rules placed around the body in Christian culture to keep us out of danger? Do you believe they are helpful or unhelpful?
3. The author asserts that "our bodies are the very focus of the story of God" (p. 75) and that we cannot be human without a body. What does she mean?
4. In using the terms *sarx* and *soma* in the New Testament, Paul is using terms without implying that either one is good or bad. How have the words "flesh" and "body" come to have moral implications?
5. While our bodies are the image of the invisible God, we regularly experience pain, betrayal, illness and death in our bodies. What does the author suggest we do with this seeming contradiction?
6. On page 117, Owens implies that we can discern how comfortable we are with our bodies by how we make space for those whose bodies are different from our own. Do you find this to be a helpful tool in discerning your own comfort level with your body?
7. Do you believe that the healing touch that the woman with the issue of blood received from Jesus in John 5 is within our power to give to others today? Why or why not?
8. Owens writes, "Most of us have spent so long trying to silence or manipulate our bodies that the messages they have to give us are muted or mixed" (p. 183). How do we silence or manipulate our bodies? What are the muted or mixed messages?
9. Chapter 11 asserts that our sexuality can be redeemed and that our sexual desires can point us toward God. Do you find this idea compelling? How so?
10. "Receive what you are, the body of Christ" jolts the author into awareness of what's happening in the Eucharist (p. 231). How are our bodies part of the body of Christ?

THE FIGHT

A Practical Handbook for Christian Living

John White

"As you enter the Christian life, you may have periods of darkness or of doubt. You may encounter painful struggle and discouragement. But there will also be moments of exultation and glory. And most important of all, you will become free."

There is joy and triumph in the Christian life. But the victory can come through struggle. John White knows this balance and gives us the encouragement to persevere. This is his classic guide to the basic areas of Christian living we wrestle with throughout our lives: faith, prayer, temptation, evangelism, guidance, Bible study, fellowship and work. White offers new Christians sound first steps and older Christians refreshing insights into the struggles and joys of freedom in Christ.

"If praying, studying the Bible, getting guidance, getting along with fellow Christians, witnessing, and the like are struggles for you, here's your book."

Christianity Today

ABOUT THE AUTHOR: John White (1924–2002) is the author of more than twenty-five books as well as numerous articles and study guides. A much sought-after speaker, he lectured around the world at churches, conferences and leadership events and planted a Vineyard church in Vancouver, British Columbia. He also served as associate professor of psychiatry at the University of Manitoba and as pastor of Church of the Way.

◆ QUESTIONS

1. White describes a time when he felt "guilty, depressed and cheated" after failing to pray early in the morning for two full hours (p. 21). Share a time when you made a goal for yourself that was not realistic.

2. "We were designed for fellowship with God, and without that fellowship we ache in emptiness. He himself planted the longing there, a longing all of us share" (p. 22). How might this idea change our attitude about prayer from one of duty to one of desire?

3. "You are a witness whether you want to be one or not. Either you are a good witness or a poor one" (p. 74). What prevents you from acting as a signpost for Jesus Christ in the lives of those around you?

4. Satan is referred to as the tempter, the accuser, the deceiver and the devourer. What did you learn about your relationship to the Evil One in chapter 5?

5. If faith is measured not by a "mystical inner state", as White suggests, but rather by concrete actions in response to God, how would you measure your faith?

6. How are faith and willpower different (pp. 104-105)?

7. According to White, what does faith look like in the midst of pain? What does it look like for you?

8. "It is not God's prime aim to make your family nice for you to live with" (p. 123). What does White say is God's prime aim for our relationships?

9. Many people interact with God as though "his favorite word is 'No' and his favorite pastime, doing without" (p. 148). How would you describe your assumptions of God when asking for guidance?

10. It is debated whether the process of sanctification is a passive one or an active one. White suggests a paradox in which both are true. Where does your own growth process fall on the spectrum from passive to active?

11. According to the book, how are work, joy, and satisfaction connected (pp. 203-214)?

12. White ends by praying the words of 2 Timothy 4:6-8 for us. What habits do you hope to create in order to make these words so?

FORGOTTEN GIRLS

Stories of Hope and Courage

Expanded Edition

Kay Marshall Strom and Michele Rickett
Foreword by Lynne Hybels

2014 IVP Readers' Choice Award Winner

Think of the little girls you know: your daughter, a niece, a friend's child. Then think about this: little girls are tossed away every day.

All over the world, women and girls face troubles such as starvation, displacement, illiteracy, sexual exploitation and abuse. Moved by the plight of these neglected girls, advocates Kay Marshall Strom and Michele Rickett took a trip across continents to interview girls and to partner with ministries working to help females in some of the most difficult places in the world. These pages hold those girls' stories: stories of deep pain and suffering, inspiring courage, and incredible hope.

"I guarantee that if you read this book, your heart will be broken—which is why you must read this book."

Lynne Hybels, advocate for global engagement, Willow Creek Community Church

ABOUT THE AUTHORS: A professional writer based in Eugene, Oregon, Kay Marshall Strom has written more than thirty books. She now partners with her husband (Daniel Kline) as Kline, Strom International, Inc., and together they have spoken to over 100,000 people in more than twenty countries.

Michele Rickett is founder and president of She Is Safe, an international ministry mobilizing advocates to equip women against poverty, oppression, exploitation and spiritual darkness. Based in Atlanta, Georgia, she is also coauthor (with husband Daniel) of a Bible study course called *Ordinary Women* and a contributing author to *A Celebration of Women.*

◆ QUESTIONS

1. Lynne Hybels writes in the forward that social scientists consider the well-being of women to be the truest indicator of the health of a culture or country. On page 15 statistics are given for the plight of women and children. How did you respond to these statements?
2. Part 1 covers issues of gendercide, child sacrifice, abandonment and hunger, which represent a host of challenges to the very survival of little girls. Which story is most memorable to you? Why?
3. Were you surprised that education was identified as the greatest need for girls? Why do you think education can make such a difference? In what ways does educating a girl affect the future for boys and men?
4. Sex trafficking of girls is rampant, especially in Eastern Europe and Asia. Were you aware that it occurs in the United States, Canada and Great Britain? Are there any indications that sex trafficking is happening in your city or state?
5. Girls are often sexually exploited under the guise of "marriage." Work marriage, hidden marriage and tiny hut marriage, even kidnapping are condoned and even encouraged by family members. How can you empathize with the families and the girls that are victims?
6. Which fact about the effects of war was the most staggering to you? What are the most difficult issues for mothers in war-torn areas?
7. Part 5 tells the spiritual journey of the abused girls. How could it be difficult for these girls to accept believing the good news? What might attract them the most?
8. How would you explain God's purposes in allowing abuse and exploitation?
9. One author asks, "Why do you think we Americans are more hesitant to help the victims of man-made disasters, such as sex trafficking of children, than the victims of natural disasters, such as earthquakes or tsunamis?" Of the answers she received (p. 162), which might you be inclined to listen to to avoid taking action?
10. It's hard not to be so overwhelmed by the tragedy of the stories that we are paralyzed into inaction. As a group, review the action items from each chapter and identify one thing you each can do.

A Conversation with . . .
Kay Marshall Strom and Michele Rickett

Forgotten Girls **chronicles the painful stories of abuse and persecution around the world. How have you been affected through meeting these young girls and gathering their stories?**

Michele: My faith has been strengthened by the resilience of these girls, and the commitment of our coworkers on the ground. I would say that my patience has been severely tested. Just when I thought I had heard the absolute worst that someone could do to a child, we would learn of an even deeper abuse, neglect or torture. I groan with Habakkuk, "How long, OLord . . . why do you make me look at injustice?" God answers, "Write this down, so a herald may run with it. For the revelation awaits an appointed time; it speaks of the end and it will not prove false." My faith is firmly placed that one day everything will be set right, and in the meantime, we have the privilege of being those heralds inviting people to join the resistance and intervene for the most vulnerable human beings on the planet: little girls.

Kay: Sometimes it seems that if enough money is waved around, no one can be trusted. And then we meet those who, in God's name, stand up against the evil. We meet those who risk everything to stand in the gap on the girls' behalf, and my faith is restored manyfold. God is still in control. But he chooses to give us responsibility. And he requires that we champion the cause of justice, that we love mercy and that, as we do it, our stance is one of walking humbly with our God.

What is most needed for changing the lives of these young girls?

Michele: Education is one of the three most powerful things we see that makes a tremendous difference for girls, women and the next generation. The most powerful life change comes from a holistic approach: education plus good nutrition plus skill training—economic empowerment—plus spiritual life in Christ.

Kay: Everywhere we went, when we asked leaders what it was that would bring hope to the next generation, the answer was education. Certainly it is extremely difficult to educate a hungry, malnourished child, or a sick one. We must care for those pressing physical needs. But to tend to the physical needs without education is to miss the chance for tomorrow. As one ministry leader in India said: if a girl learns to read, eternity opens up to her because she can read the Bible. In fact, many Christian women first discover the value of education for that very reason: they want to read the Bible.

What unique, positive lessons or values did you learn from the cultures you experienced?

Michele: Hospitality is a deep value from Africa through the Middle East and across Asia. Visitors are happily given something refreshing to eat and drink, even when families have very little for themselves. Special regard for the elderly is a common value in the places we visited too. We recently sat in the Sahara desert in a West African village and watched the young, strong men offer the best of a goat to the elderly chief and shaman. We have much to learn.

Kay: I was deeply touched by the strength and resilience we saw demonstrated so many times and in so many places. I have also been greatly moved by their emphasis on developing a relationship. We sat in people's homes and drank tea, we ate with them at their tables. People valued what we had to offer, but even more they valued the relationship. One father said, "Other people come and give to us. But you came and drank tea in my house. You sat with us and showed us God."

You encourage readers to take action. What is the best way to stay connected to these girls and their issues, especially since they can seem so far removed from our own lives in the United States?

Michele: The best way to keep passion alive is to invest some time in a solution. We have found that when people band together for prayer, planning and advocacy, they are much better able to keep the flames alive. One can always subscribe for updates on the hard-hitting issues for girls at sistersinservice.org or resistthedarkness.org.

Kay: First of all, it is important to stay updated on the issues. Often, though, people are so moved they want to jump in and do something themselves. But in these difficult situations the very best thing to do is to connect with an organization that is already at work on the frontlines and help them do what they are already set up to do.

THE GIFT OF BEING YOURSELF

The Sacred Call to Self-Discovery

David G. Benner

Much is said in Christian circles about knowing God. But Christians throughout the ages have agreed that there cannot be deep knowledge of God without deep knowledge of the self. Discerning your true self is inextricably related to discerning God's purposes for you. Paradoxically, the more you become like Christ, the more you become authentically yourself.

In this profound exploration of Christian identity, psychologist and spiritual director David G. Benner illuminates the spirituality of self-discovery. He exposes the false selves that you may hide behind and calls you to discover the true self that emerges from your uniqueness in Christ. Freeing you from illusions about yourself, Benner shows that self-understanding leads to the fulfillment of your God-given destiny and vocation.

"With empathy and insight [Benner] demonstrates that the two great tasks of life—knowing God and knowing ourselves—converge into a single adventure as we are drawn into the arms of our loving God."

Mark R. McMinn, Rech Professor of Psychology, Wheaton College

ABOUT THE AUTHOR: David G. Benner (PhD, York University) is Emeritus Distinguished Professor of Psychology and Spirituality at Richmont Graduate University in Atlanta, Georgia. A depth psychologist, spiritual director and retreat leader, Benner has written and edited many books, including the *Baker Encyclopedia of Psychology and Counseling* and *Care of Souls*. He is the founding executive editor of the journal *Conversations*.

◆ QUESTIONS

1. What was your definition of your "true self" before you read this book? Did it change?
2. "A tulip knows exactly what it is," the author writes. Do you believe that there is a unique way of being for you that is "as natural and deeply congruent as the life of the tulip" (pp. 14-15)?
3. What are the consequences of not believing that every person is "of immense value to God" (p. 16)?
4. The author asks, "What would you identify as the most important thing for your existence and well-being?" How would you answer this question (p. 19)?
5. The author writes, "Unless we spend as much time looking at God as we spend looking at our self, our knowing of our self will simply draw us further and further into an abyss of self-fixation" (p. 23). How can we combat this temptation?
6. Like the pastor the author describes, have you ever believed something about God without knowing it for yourself (p. 23)? What is the difference?
7. What can make us "afraid to look deeply" at ourselves and at God?
8. God knows us fully, yet loves and accepts us as we are. If we know this, why can it still be difficult to feel the same way about ourselves?
9. Which personality type in the Enneagram do you most identify with (pp. 68-70)? How can this knowledge help you face your own sins?
10. Which is more difficult to accept—the reality of your sinful nature or the fact that you are deeply loved by God?
11. In what ways can you personally "discern and dismantle" your false self (p. 78)?
12. How are your identity, your calling and your job both related and distinct?
13. Why is "the way of the true self . . . always the way of humility" (p. 98)?
14. In his conclusion, the author writes, "It remains to make these big ideals practical" (p. 105). What kind of steps will you take to apply the ideas in this book and move beyond them?

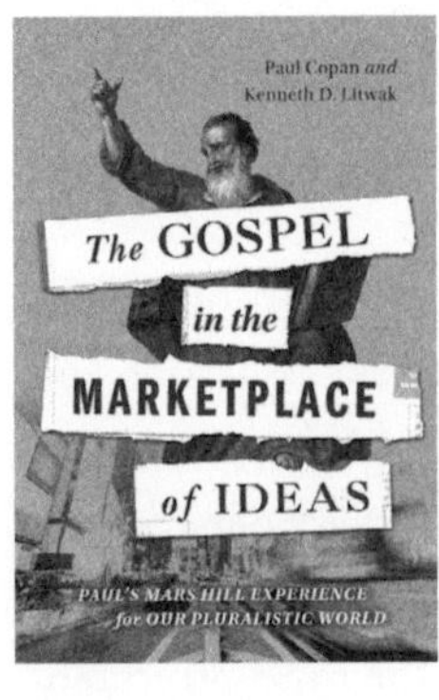

THE GOSPEL IN THE MARKETPLACE OF IDEAS

Paul's Mars Hill Experience for Our Pluralistic World

Paul Copan and Kenneth D. Litwak

Our world is multicultural, multireligious, multiphilosophical. How can Christians engage in communicating across worldviews in this pluralistic and often relativistic society?

When Paul visited Athens, he found an equally multicultural and multireligious setting. Seeking to embolden the church's witness in today's society, philosopher Paul Copan and New Testament scholar Kenneth Litwak reveal how Paul's speech to the Athenians (found in Acts 17) provides a practical model for Christians today. They uncover the cultural and religious background of this key episode in the apostle's career and encourage believers to winsomely challenge the idols of our time, pointing contemporary Athenians to Christ.

> *"In this thought-provoking book, a Christian apologist and a New Testament scholar join forces to read Luke's famous story of Paul on Mars Hill, and the result is as compelling as it is remarkable."*
>
> **Joel B. Green, Fuller Theological Seminary**

ABOUT THE AUTHORS: Paul Copan is the Pledger Family Chair of Philosophy and Ethics at Palm Beach Atlantic University. He has written and edited several books, including *Creation Out of Nothing* and *Will the Real Jesus Please Stand Up?* He has also served with Ravi Zacharias International Ministries and taught at Trinity International University.

Kenneth D. Litwak is adjunct professor of New Testament studies at Azusa Pacific University and Asbury Seminary. He is the author of *Echoes of Scripture in Luke-Acts: Telling the History of God's People Intertextually*.

◆ QUESTIONS

1. The book explains that some scholars believe Paul viewed his address at Athens as a failure. Do you think this is a valid argument? What is the evidence for and against this viewpoint (pp. 20-26)?
2. Does your life reflect any of the influential worldviews of our modern day Athens, like postmodernism, relativism or scientism? How (pp. 49-63)?
3. What makes the Christian worldview distinct from the other worldviews of today, just as the gospel was distinct from the Athenian worldview?
4. Why do the authors argue it is important to understand or "exegete" culture when communicating your faith (p. 75)?
5. Paul uses biblical truth as the foundation for his Areopagus speech, but he does not directly quote Scripture. What do you think of this method of sharing the gospel (pp. 118-120)?
6. How can you give people in your life space to wrestle with profound philosophical and spiritual questions (p. 153)?
7. The authors say that the biggest step for postmoderns in their faith journeys is coming to trust Christians. What causes this mistrust, and how can Christians overcome their misgivings (p. 154)?
8. Money, technology, relationships, knowledge. Like the numerous gods of Athens, what other modern day idols take the place of the one true God (pp. 156-157)?
9. Think about your work, family and social context. What marketplace ideas common to these settings can be used as a starting point in sharing your faith?
10. The authors provide a hypothetical progression of steps to faith. It's a slow process. Does this change your expectations for how quickly people should respond to the gospel message, especially considering that even Paul sometimes didn't bring large numbers of people to faith at one time (p. 151)?
11. Go back and re-read Paul's speech once you have finished the book. How do his words hit you differently now that you understand the historical context, the audience and Paul's use of rhetoric?

JUSTICE AWAKENING

How You and Your Church Can Help End Human Trafficking

Eddie Byun

2014 IVP Readers' Choice Award Winner

The realities of modern-day slavery can seem daunting, and sometimes it can feel like we should leave it to the professionals. But fighting for justice is not something we have to outsource to others. Every Christian and every church has a part to play.

Pastor and activist Eddie Byun provides biblical foundations for understanding God's heart for justice and the oppressed. He offers practical, on-the-ground steps that any believer or church can take, from youth groups to men's ministries, orphan care ministries to short-term and long-term missions. Discover what you can do to be part of the solution. And join God's movement for freedom and justice for all.

"This book beats with the passionate heart of God and gives practical ways for us to be the hands of God to those who are enslaved."

Mike Bickle, director of the International House of Prayer of Kansas City

"Pastor Eddie doesn't just share what's wrong with the world—he provides a road map to get active in making things right. His great passion for the church and for the most vulnerable people in our world fills each page."

Gary Haugen, president and CEO of International Justice Mission

ABOUT THE AUTHOR: Eddie Byun (DMin, Gordon-Conwell Theological Seminary) is lead pastor at Onnuri English Ministry (OEM), the English-speaking ministry of Onnuri Community Church in Seoul, Korea. He fights against modern-day slavery through HOPE Be Restored, a ministry of OEM.

◆ QUESTIONS

1. When did you first hear about human trafficking and how did it make you feel?
2. Do you feel the church should be more involved in establishing justice or is it better left to organizations with that as their primary mission?
3. Which verse describing God's definition of justice stood out to you the most? Does your church preach on the subject of justice?
4. The author writes about the end-time judgment in regard to justice (pp. 48-51). His conclusion is that God expects us to partner with him in establishing justice. What do you think is the connection between the cross, the final judgment and our actions for justice today?
5. Human trafficking has many forms. Which group of victims or type of trafficking grieves you the most? Were there any that you were unaware of and would like to learn more about?
6. The author gives his reasons why the church should lead the cause (chap. 4). Has he convinced you? In your own words, why do you think the church must lead?
7. In chapter 5, a comprehensive guide focusing on teams, pastors, individuals and other ministries is given listing what the church and members can do. Which idea sounded like a good place for your church to begin? Which idea convicted you the most?
8. After each chapter is a prayer guide. How has praying about justice and the church affected you?
9. After reading this book, what is your next step in helping to end human trafficking? Who will you share your next step with?

LESSONS IN BELONGING FROM A CHURCH-GOING COMMITMENT PHOBE

Erin S. Lane
Foreword by Parker J. Palmer

There was a time when being a part of a church was not a decision you made but a reality you inhabited. But today, belonging to the church has become a lost art, especially for millennials whose church experience is often summed up in one word: *none.*

Erin Lane's church experience might be better described in two words: "It's complicated." With earnest persistence, Erin practiced the hard (and often surprising) lessons of community. Her story is an invitation to reclaim God's promise of inclusion and live like we belong to one another.

"If you are looking for yet another sanitized treatise on the joys of Jesus and his church, do not open this book. But if you want real talk about real dilemmas in our own broken lives and in the broken life of the church, this book is for you."

From the foreword by Parker J. Palmer

"Plenty of folks want Jesus but not the church. . . . In this raw, winsome book, Erin cuts through the fluff. She has seen the funk of Christianity—but she has fallen in love with a beautiful God whose grace overshadows the funk of the church."

Shane Claiborne, author of *The Irresistible Revolution*

ABOUT THE AUTHOR: Erin S. Lane works for the Seattle-based non-profit Center for Courage & Renewal as an assistant program director for Clergy & Congregational Leader Programs. She has a masters of theological studies degree from Duke Divinity School and is coeditor of *Talking Taboo,* an anthology of writing from young Christian women on the intersection of faith and gender.

Read Erin's blog at holyhellions.com.

◆ QUESTIONS

1. Erin Lane reminds us that "belonging is a lost art" (p. 10). Prior to reading this book, how did you react to the word *belonging*?
2. A group of eighth graders made a distinction between fitting in and belonging: "Fitting in means I have to be like you. Belonging means I get to be me" (p. 25). Why is this distinction so important? Do you think "fitting in" or "belonging" is experienced more within churches?
3. Trust is often thought of as being gained or lost. What might it mean for you to believe that trust is something that happens *with* you rather than *to* you (p. 73)?
4. In lesson 3, Erin names habits like regularly showing up at worship, accepting invitations and learning the names of strangers. What habits help you sustain your involvement at church?
5. Erin decided to revert to her maiden name after marriage. How did you respond to that? How does your name make you feel like you do or don't belong?
6. Erin writes, "Where other institutions ask us to bring our best self, put on our can-do face and save the world one problem at a time, the church allows us to start from the ground of our true being" (p. 121). How can you help yourself and others experience church this way?
7. In an effort to practice vulnerability Erin speaks her need. What one need do you currently have? Does speaking that need feel like a risk?
8. What groups or organizations are you a member of? How is membership in the local church distinct? Why have you joined or not joined a local church?
9. "It's hard to know what the labels mean: *evangelical, emergent, conservative, liberal, progressive, mainline, missional*; they seem so contextual, geographical, even nonsensical at times" (p. 148). Are labels helpful or hurtful? Why?
10. How have you discerned the balance between choosing a faith community in which you are both stretched and nurtured?
11. "Belonging happens when we choose to give ourselves away, saying, 'Take. Eat. If you'll have me, I belong to you'" (p. 177). How has reading this book changed your understanding of belonging?

A Conversation with . . . *Erin S. Lane*

What made you want to write a book about not being a "none"?

Erin Lane: Because I'm a contrarian. Jokes aside, my generation often defines ourselves by what we are against rather than what we are about. I wanted to write a book that explored why anyone my age would be "about" belonging to the church and the gifts we could offer it if we chose to stick around.

You write that disillusionment is a good thing. Why do you think this is so, and what role can the church play in this?

Erin: Disillusionment has gotten a bad rap. We use it as a way to describe disappointment. I want to recover its most basic meaning as the process of being "stripped" or "freed" from our illusions. Illusions are what keep us from living in reality, and if there's one thing that's been made clear to me in writing this book, it's that God's reality is better than any fiction I know. It follows then that the church should be a place where we regularly go to get our "reality check," a place where we can act out who we really are and to whom we really belong.

Why do you think belonging is so important for the millennial generation? What do you hope they'll take away from reading about your journey?

Erin: I think belonging is so important to my generation because we feel overwhelmed by the world and the need to find our place in it. We have more options for connecting with one another than ever and more pressure to make the most of them. Further, the institutions that previously brokered these connections are losing influence in places like North America. The path to belonging is more confusing than ever. My hope is that readers will feel less alone after reading about my own foibles in belonging and take some small steps—the lessons of belonging, if you will—toward realizing their identity in a community of faith.

How does your spiritual story, from being raised as a Catholic to being a Methodist pastor's wife, play a role in how you personally found a place where you feel at home?

Erin: I don't have a lot of hope that I'd be committed to the church today if my faith identity weren't so tied to the lives of those I love most. Granted, I'm not someone who really likes the "church as family" metaphor since I think encountering strangers is one of the best parts about going to church. But having a familial connection to the church helps a commitment phobe like me narrow her options and focus on choosing one place at a time to call home. Still, I don't think I'll ever feel at home in any one tradition. I'm a wanderer, and instead of seeing that as a character flaw (or symptomatic of my generation), I see that now as the gift of going where the Spirit leads.

What's the most important thing you'd say to someone who is spiritual but can't find the motivation to be at church each Sunday?

Erin: I'd say, "Me, too." I can't find the motivation to be at church each Sunday either but I still try to do it. Going to church has to depend on something more than motivation. It has to be a habit that you practice—or want to practice—because at some point you had a revelation that this is where real life is found. A mentor of mine has a quote on her desk that reads, "Discipline is remembering what you want." Do you want to go to church each Sunday? If not, I can't convince you. But if so, I'll be right there with you.

What's the number one thing you'd say to folks already in the pews trying to bring in this "none" generation?

Erin: I'd say, "Be yourselves." There's nothing more important for the "none" generation than finding a community that's authentic, transparent and honest. Don't try to be something else than you are, but also know that you might have to stretch your comfort zone to welcome the unprecedented diversity of my generation.

How do you think readers can find belonging through activism and outreach programs beyond the church doors?

Erin: Each of us belongs to a variety of communities in which we find identity and purpose. Although I consider the local church to be "ground zero" for shaping my beliefs on belonging, the nonprofit I work for—the Center for Courage & Renewal—has been more influential in my understanding of how we practice belonging. I think the church has a lot to learn from life outside its doors and can only benefit from those of us with enough wherewithal to journey between the two.

LISTEN IN

Building Faith and Friendship Through Conversations That Matter

Rachael Crabb, Sonya Reeder and Diana Calvin

Foreword & Afterword by Larry Crabb

How do we have conversations that matter?

In these pages Rachael Crabb and two of her friends in ministry take up this question in a creative and informative way, providing model dialogues with one another exploring the deep issues of their lives. You will be intrigued and informed by learning from their journeys, but most importantly you will learn how you can start similar conversations with your friends. Come along and listen in.

"Listening in to these richly nuanced conversations is more than just fascinating. It offers the hope that any woman can open her inner self with courage, pursue her friends with kind curiosity and discover beauty hidden within her story."

Nancy Groom, author of *Risking Intimacy*

"I want to be the kind of friend that Rachael, Sonya and Diana are to one another and I'm thankful that they have generously let us listen in."

Emily P. Freeman, author of *A Million Little Ways* and *Grace for the Good Girl*

ABOUT THE AUTHORS: Rachael Crabb, Sonya Reeder and Diana Calvin are friends whose relationships span two generations and 850 miles. Based in Denver, Colorado, Crabb is an author and ministry consultant who has spoken at conferences and retreats worldwide for over twenty years. Reeder, a licensed professional counselor in Longview, Texas, has operated a private practice for twenty-three years and Calvin serves as connections minister at Trinity Fellowship Church in Richardson, Texas.

◆ QUESTIONS

1. The goal of *Listen In* is to help women have conversations that matter—not fluff as Sonya puts it. Describe your usual conversations with women. How would you rate the depth of conversation?
2. The authors identified five key ingredients to guide conversations (pp. 16-18). Which of these would make the most impact in your conversations?
3. The book format is transcribed conversations. What did you think about listening in to their conversations? Were you surprised by any of the comments the authors said to one another?
4. A death word is explained as an action, phrase or attitude toward you that incorrectly defines who you are (p. 34). Was "death words" a new concept to you? When have you experienced the power of negative words said against you?
5. In each woman's story they uncover a word to describe themselves. What is one word you would use to describe yourself?
6. In Rachael's story she discovered she protected her core self through outspokenness. What are other ways women protect their inner selves?
7. Sonya struggled with "being different." How do you think God has made you unlike everyone else, and how can you help others to discover what makes them unique?
8. The stories the authors share from their past affect their lives today. How can you encourage one another to look at our pasts with compassion and live more fully in the present?
9. Diana describes her competency as an addiction. Was this surprising to you? What are other positive traits that we might be addicted to?
10. How might sharing your own experience offer helpful feedback in a conversation with a friend? When do you use it as a way to talk about yourself or to get the focus on you?
11. Which woman's story did you resonate with the most? Is there a question you wish had been asked of one of the women?
12. What man in your life would you like to read this book?

REDEEMING SEX

Naked Conversations About Sexuality and Spirituality

Debra Hirsch

Foreword by Gabe Lyons

Nothing has exposed the gap between the church and the broader society quite like the cultural argument over sexuality. Relationships, identities, orientations and even seemingly straightforward concepts such as gender have cut battle lines between the church and the world.

There is hope, however. Debra Hirsch has seen it firsthand—in meaningful lifelong relationships with LGBT friends and neighbors, in Christian fellowships, and in movements that have held a concern for people created in God's image and a high view of the Bible's teaching on sexuality in constructive tension. Discover a holistic, biblical vision of sex and gender that honors God and offers good news to the world.

"I'm so grateful to Deb Hirsch for writing the best book on this conversation I have read. . . . It is prophetic, profound, candid, transparent and should be read by every Christian. It will challenge you to the core."

Christine Caine, director, Equip & Empower Ministries

"Redeeming Sex *pulls no punches yet graciously guides us toward the heart of God in our human sexuality."*

Hugh Halter, author of *Flesh*

ABOUT THE AUTHOR: Debra Hirsch has led churches and ministries among young adults, the poor and the LGBT community in Australia and America for over twenty years. She is coauthor (with Alan Hirsch) of *Untamed: Reactivating a Missional Form of Discipleship*. She serves on the leadership team of the Forge Missions Training Network and on the steering team for the Missio Alliance.

◆ QUESTIONS

1. What messages have you heard about sexuality at church? Do you feel that your questions about how to live faithfully as a sexual being have been answered? Why or why not?
2. Hirsch says: "Properly understood and expressed, our sexuality can be an amazing access point for people to rediscover God." What do you believe Christians have to offer the broader culture on the topic of sexuality?
3. Do you find Hirsch's description of sexuality and spirituality as two sides of the same coin to be helpful? If so, how?
4. Why do you think that people tend to create a hierarchy of sins within the church? What might be done to change that?
5. What can we learn from looking at Jesus as our model of sexuality?
6. Of the eight "*fun*damentals" of sex, which one(s) made the most sense to you? Were there any statements that you disagreed with?
7. How is a person's gender related to his or her biological sex?
8. Do you have acquaintances or relationships with people who are gay or transgender? How has this affected your understanding of sexuality?
9. Determining what Scripture says about the God-given boundaries of sexual behavior requires discernment. How might a "redemptive movement hermeneutic" be of assistance here?
10. If sexual orientation is somewhat fluid—as Deb's and Richard's stories attest—what are the implications?
11. What are the effects of seeing people as first and foremost created in the image of God rather than first and foremost as sinners?
12. Do you think that the church has placed too much emphasis on the nuclear family? Why or why not?
13. What can we learn from the way Jesus interacts with the woman caught in adultery?
14. What does living out our sexuality faithfully entail?
15. How can we move toward a more charitable and loving way of engaging with those who have orientations different from our own?

THE RELATIONAL SOUL

Moving from False Self to Deep Connection

Richard Plass and James Cofield

What does loneliness tell us?

"Be it chronic or acute, slight or significant, loneliness is proof of our relational design. At the core of our being is this truth—we are *designed for* and *defined by* our relationships," the authors write. "We were born with a relentless longing to participate in the lives of others. Fundamentally, we are relational souls."

Authored by counselor Dr. Richard Plass and spiritual director James Cofield, *The Relational Soul* brings together concepts from psychology and spiritual formation. When the presence of Christ and community connects with an open soul, we witness the miracle of transformation.

"You are holding in your hands more than a book. Richard Plass and James Cofield have given us a roadmap to help us find the way to each other and to the heart of God."

Stephen W. Smith, Potter's Inn Ministry, author of *The Lazarus Life*

"The Relational Soul *provides real insight into why relationships are so essential, and yet often so aching. . . . Hope and help for healing is here!"*

Mindy Caliguire, Willow Creek Association

ABOUT THE AUTHORS: Richard Plass is president of CrossPoint Ministry where he cultivates spiritual formation in the lives of leaders. He served in pastoral ministry for twenty-five years and also as a counselor.

James Cofield is director of CrossPoint Ministry. He taught communications at Tennessee Temple University and Greek at Dallas Theological Seminary. James served as a church planter and pastor before joining CrossPoint where he offers spiritual direction and retreat leadership.

◆ QUESTIONS

1. In chapter 1, the authors describe how humans are designed for relationship. How does our understanding of God and his purposes shape our understanding of all relationships?
2. The authors list various relational patterns, claiming, "The quality and character of the programming we received early in life establishes a pattern of attachment that controls our relationships later in life" (p. 25). How much had you thought about this principle before reading this book, and how has your understanding changed?
3. How have you seen repeated patterns of reactivity in relationships around you, and how do those patterns affect the relationships (pp. 34-35)?
4. Chapter 3 explains how emotions shape our thought processes (p. 48). How can understanding the role of emotions affect your decision making and how you respond to other people?
5. Do you find the use of the term *false self* helpful in discussing behavior and relationships (chap. 4)? Why or why not?
6. The authors write, "Because of our relational design we cannot change without the presence of others" (p. 70). What examples or experiences can you share that either support or challenge this claim?
7. Why do you think having fellowship with God requires a death to self? What does this death look like (p. 76)?
8. How would you describe what it looks or feels like to live as a receptive true self (chap. 6)?
9. One of the core spiritual disciplines the authors discuss is contemplative Scripture reading (chap. 9). Have you learned about or encountered this practice in the churches or other Christian circles you've participated in? Why do you think that is?
10. In chapter 10 the authors list five characteristics of people surrendering to Christ (pp. 153-62). Did any of these stand out to you as particularly surprising or powerful?
11. What is one next step you would like to take to apply what you've discovered in *The Relational Soul*?

RENAISSANCE

The Power of the Gospel However Dark the Times

Os Guinness

We live in dark times. Are the best days of the Christian faith behind us? Is society beyond all hope of redemption and renewal?

Os Guinness declares *no*. The church can be revived to become a renewing power in our society—if we answer the call to a new Christian renaissance that challenges darkness with the hope of Christian faith.

In this hopeful appeal for cultural transformation, Guinness shares opportunities for Christians, on both local and global levels, to win back the West and contribute constructively to the human future. Hearkening back to similar pivotal points in history, Guinness encourages Christians in the quest for societal change.

"This is a profound, realistic and hopeful book that reminds us that even in the darkest times the power of the gospel can change the world."

Rebecca Manley Pippert, speaker and author of *Hope Has Its Reasons*

"For decades Os Guinness has been one of the most nuanced, realistic, yet hopeful voices calling Christians to engagement with culture. This latest volume from him should not be missed by anyone."

Tim Keller, Redeemer Presbyterian Church, New York City

ABOUT THE AUTHOR: Os Guinness (DPhil, Oxford) is the author or editor of more than thirty books, including *The Global Public Square, A Free People's Suicide, The Call, Time for Truth* and *The Case for Civility*. A frequent speaker and prominent social critic, he has addressed audiences worldwide. He founded the Trinity Forum and served as senior fellow there for fifteen years.

◆ QUESTIONS

1. What is your assessment of the church today? Do you generally feel encouraged or discouraged and why?
2. Why do you think Guinness considers himself both an optimist and a realist when it comes to a renaissance for the Christian faith?
3. Guinness talks about starting fresh with Christianity in this book; we are missionaries for today. What difference would it make to view Christianity not as in decline, but to view ourselves as missionaries to the West? What would this look like?
4. Guinness writes, "Faithful presence is not enough. It is merely the beginning. Jesus was not merely present in the world, but far, far more. He was intensely active" (p. 87). How can we model this?
5. What do you see as the great issues facing humanity in the future? How could you engage with these issues, given your individual calling?
6. What would the Western world be like if Jesus had never been born? What will it look like in the future if all Christian truths are rejected?
7. Where are Christians today in danger of usurping God's place by relying on the power of modern insights and technologies rather than on the power of God?
8. When Guinness writes we must "live in truth," what does that mean practically speaking (p. 86)?
9. In chapter 5, Guinness talks about insights of scholarship and principles of the kingdom of God. How can we relate these two things together? How do they work together?
10. How is prayer a part of revival for your life and the life of the church more broadly? How can Western Christians improve on this?
11. Reflect on your greatest Christian heroes or your favorite period in Christian history. What are the best and worst features? What does Guinness mean when he writes that our golden age is always ahead (chap. 6)?
12. As you look at the current state of the Christian church, where do you think we need to critically examine the past in order to move into the future? How will this help the renaissance for Western Christianity?

SLOW CHURCH

Cultivating Community in the Patient Way of Jesus

C. Christopher Smith and John Pattison

Foreword by Jonathan Wilson-Hartgrove

2014 IVP Readers' Choice Award Winner

Fast food. Fast cars. Fast and furious. Fast forward. Fast . . . church?

In the beginning, the church ate together, traveled together and shared in all facets of life. Centered as they were on Jesus, these seemingly mundane activities took on their own significance in the mission of God. Chris Smith and John Pattison invite us to leave franchise faith behind and enter into the ecology, economy and ethics of the kingdom of God, where people know each other well and love one another as Christ loved the church.

"In a culture that values speed and worships efficiency, Christopher Smith and John Pattison show us the graceful rhythms of fully embodied presence. . . . Food tastes better when it marinates. Church is no different."

J.R. Briggs, pastor and author of *Fail*

"This thoughtful, discerning book advocates 'slow' in faith and in life. . . . Readers eager for an evangelically paced life will pay close attention to this advocacy."

Walter Brueggemann, Columbia Theological Seminary

ABOUT THE AUTHORS: C. Christopher Smith is editor of *The Englewood Review of Books*, and a member of the Englewood Christian Church community in Indianapolis. Chris's recent work has appeared in *Books and Culture, Sojourners, The Christian Century* and *Indiana Green Living*.

John Pattison is managing editor of *CONSPIRE* magazine. Previously he served as deputy editor of the Burnside Writers Collective. A member of the National Book Critics Circle, John is the coauthor of *Besides the Bible: 100 Books that Have, Should, or Will Create Christian Culture*.

◆ QUESTIONS

1. What is most appealing to you about the concept of Slow Church?
2. In a culture that seems to prize speed above all else, how do you respond to the idea of God's patience? How might a deeper understanding of God's patience inform the ways we go about "doing church"?
3. "You can't franchise the kingdom of God" (p. 41). In what ways have you seen the "McDonaldization" of the church, with the values of efficiency, calculability, predictability or control especially championed?
4. How might a commitment to a place help create a different kind of church? If knowing a place is essential to loving a place, what are some practical ways to get to know your community better?
5. In chapter 3, the authors argue: "The greatest challenges to stability in churches today are hypermobility and individualism" (pp. 62-63). Do you agree or disagree with this assessment? Why?
6. In what ways do you find yourself formed by living in a "culture of impatience" (p. 80)?
7. According to the authors, "Our avoidance of suffering dilutes our witness to our Lord Jesus, who took our suffering upon himself in love" (p. 83). Do you agree that we need to embrace suffering as a part of our witness? If so, what might that look like?
8. In chapter 6, the authors contend: "Good work should be fundamentally understood as cooperation with God" (p. 125). How do you view the connection between your work and your faith?
9. In your experience, what makes taking a sabbath day difficult? What do we miss when we neglect to slow down and practice the sabbath?
10. "Sharing meals creates a space where the conversational life of the church can flourish" (p. 215). Do you believe that such a simple practice could transform the life of a community? Why or why not?
11. Throughout *Slow Church*, the authors suggest spiritual practices they have found helpful for slowing down and living more faithfully. If you and your group could pick one of these practices to do together, what might it be?

STARTING SOMETHING NEW

Spiritual Direction for Your God-Given Dream

Beth A. Booram

Do you have a dream? Do you long to change your lifestyle or vocation, or to start a new business or nonprofit ministry? Do you find yourself wondering, *How do I know for sure that this dream is from God and for me? And what in the world do I do with it?*

Drawing from her own life-changing experience of realizing a dream, spiritual director Beth Booram has written this book to guide you through the spiritual process of defining and acting on the idea stirring within you. Interviews are included from people who have courageously embraced a God-prompted idea, such as Chris Smith, Phileena Heuertz and Randy Reese, to add further vision and insight for those who are actively tending a God-given dream.

> *"This new book by Beth Booram is a wonderful gift to all of us who dare to dream but are unsure what to do with those dreams. . . . Hold this book in one hand and your dream in the other and watch as the Spirit leads you forward!"*
>
> **David G. Benner, author of *The Gift of Being Yourself***

ABOUT THE AUTHOR: Beth Booram is the cofounder and director of Sustainable Faith Indy, an urban retreat center in Indianapolis, where she leads the School of Spiritual Direction and offers individual and group spiritual direction. Beth is the author or coauthor of several books including *Awaken Your Senses, Picturing the Face of Jesus* and *The Wide Open Spaces of God*. She spent sixteen years on staff with Campus Crusade for Christ and has served in several pastoral roles within the local church, including leading a weekly women's ministry of more than five-hundred women.

◆ QUESTIONS

1. In chapter 1, Beth Booram asks us to pay attention to our desires and our prayers. What do you normally do with your desire and discontent? How do you think God views our desires?
2. Beth says that "values might be the raw material of a God-given dream" (p. 44). How do personal values give shape to the concrete details of our dreams?
3. Beth talks about a "wall of resistance" that we meet when we begin to pay serious attention to our dreams (p. 52). What can make it difficult for us to welcome our dreams?
4. In chapter 4, Beth encourages calling a "clearness committee" for discernment. Why is discerning a dream in community important?
5. Beth discusses how our dreams and our work are shaped by our unique, God-given personalities (chap. 6). Why should you celebrate the unique qualities that you and others have?
6. Making choices at a crossroads is part of the journey in working out a dream. Beth says, "If a ways down the road something about it doesn't seem right—it's okay to change your mind" (p. 105). Changing your mind can be disappointing and painful. What makes it okay?
7. In chapter 9, Beth discusses the "crucible of waiting." What does it feel like to wait? How do you usually occupy a season of waiting?
8. Describe the role of "holy indifference" in the process of waiting (p. 113). What do you think our culture tells us in contrast? What can happen if we don't let go of our dreams?
9. When a dream dies, how do you picture yourself and God? Reflect on the epigraph to chapter 10: "The seed must rest in the earth. We must allow the Christ-life to grow in us in rest. Our whole being must fold upon Christ's rest in us, as the earth folds upon the seed." How does the image of the seed feel in comparison?
10. In chapter 14, Beth discusses a "rule of life," or daily rhythm. What is a rule of life, and how can it help sustain you in your work?
11. What small dream has this book nudged you toward?

TEACH US TO WANT

Longing, Ambition & the Life of Faith

Jen Pollock Michel

Foreword by Katelyn Beaty

2015 Christianity Today Book of the Year!

As Christians, we're squeamish about desire. Isn't wanting sinful and selfish? Aren't we supposed to follow God's will rather than insisting upon our own?

The story of each person is a story of want—desires unmet, hopes dashed, passions pursued and ambitions fulfilled. Our wants cannot be ignored. Jen Pollock Michel guides us on a journey of understanding who we are when we want and reintroduces us to a God who gives us the desires of our hearts. The disciples asked Jesus to "Teach us to pray." This book asks, "Teach us to want."

"Seriously, one of the most beautiful nonfiction books I have ever read."

Bethany Jenkins, founder, The Park Forum

"Who has not wrestled with the tensions between what we desire and what (we think) God desires? Michel has brilliantly lit a way through our own dark, tangled brambles. I've been waiting for this book for a long time."

Leslie Leyland Fields, author of *Forgiving Our Fathers and Mothers*

ABOUT THE AUTHOR: Jen Pollock Michel is a regular contributor for *Christianity Today's* Her.meneutics and writes for *Today in the Word*, published by Moody Bible Institute. Jen earned her BA in French from Wheaton College and her MA in literature from Northwestern University. She lives in Toronto, Canada, with her husband and five children.

Follow Jen on Twitter (@jenpmichel) or find her at jenpollockmichel.com.

◆ QUESTIONS

1. Jen Michel describes her mistaken theology of desire: "I have wanted to believe that desire is bad, that I am bad for wanting" (chap. 1). Are these notions about desire common in the church? If so, why?
2. Jen notes: "The simple question, 'What do I want?' can lead to important change. . . . Ignoring our desires may serve as the convenient way we remain ignorant and resist change" (p. 43). How might the exploration of desire affect profound spiritual transformation?
3. Jen always returns to grace, claiming that by virtue of God's steadfast and forgiving love, he rescues us from our faithless desires. Is this the abuse of grace to which Paul refers in Romans 6:1, where he asks, "Are we to continue in sin that grace may abound?" If not, what might be the difference?
4. Learning the language of holy desire is something that happens when we keep company with other Christians. As Hebrews 10:24-25 says, "And let us consider how we may spur one another toward love and good deeds, not giving up meeting together, as some are in the habit of doing, but encouraging one another." Why are God's people so critical to navigating the terrain of our own heart's desires?
5. The author claims that her stories of loss are critically important to a biblical discussion of desire. Do you agree that loss and disappointment are necessary for a life of holy desire? Why or why not?
6. The book hangs loosely on the structure of the Lord's Prayer, suggesting that holy desire is formed by practices of Scripture reading, prayer, petition, confession and community. How do we reconcile the importance of God's grace and our intentional practices, particularly for the renovation of our desires?
7. The author suggests that prayer, at its best, is brave and authentic. We should learn to meet God in our "doubt and desire, praise and perplexity, fear and failure" (p. 120). Is this view of prayer supported by Scripture? In your experience, is it welcome in our churches?
8. In the final chapter, the author suggests two biblical fruits of holy desire from Psalm 20: petitions and plans. What does desire look like without holy petitions and plans? What do petitions and plans look like without holy desire?

TEN

Words of Life for an Addicted, Compulsive, Cynical, Divided and Worn-Out Culture

Sean Gladding

To most people living in today's world, the Ten Commandments represent archaic rules dictated by a taskmaster God, meant for a society long gone. Many see them as irrelevant, even unattainable, today. But what if we're not that different from those who gathered around Moses as he handed down God's Ten Words to his people? What if they were never meant to be a set of rules, but instead a promise of a covenant relationship?

In *Ten,* Sean Gladding invites you into the story of John, a pastor who spends his mornings in a local coffee shop, as he engages the viewpoints of regular people who wonder at the relevance and meaning of those Ten Words today. Sit in on their lively, heartfelt conversations as they tackle each Word over a cup of coffee and realize the hope of God's promises to his chosen people—yesterday, today and forever.

"You've never heard the Ten Commandments taught quite like this."

Michael Frost, author of *The Shaping of Things to Come* and *Exiles*

"Sean Gladding has taken his love for God and love of the other and invited each of us into a deeper spiritual devotion through the pages of Ten.*"*

Tony Kriz, author of *Welcome to the Table* and *Neighbors and Wise Men*

ABOUT THE AUTHOR: Originally hailing from Norwich, England, Sean Gladding has made his home in the United States for the last two decades, where he has served as pastor with college students, in church plants and as part of the new monasticism. He is the author of the *The Story of God, the Story of Us*.

◆ QUESTIONS

1. The Ten Commandments are not often talked about or studied. Why do you think that is?
2. Are the Ten Commandments relevant to you in your day-to-day life? Why or why not?
3. The book begins with a discussion on the Ten Commandments. What do they represent to you? Is that more important than their actual content?
4. Of the reasons given for keeping or disregarding the Ten Commandments, which one resonated most with you?
5. Which character do you identify with the most? Which the least? Why?
6. Do you think these characters are a likely group to have a "religious" discussion? Why or why not?
7. Why is talking about matters of religion so tricky?
8. What's the most diverse group of people with which you've had a significant discussion? How did you come to be part of that group?
9. Which commandment discussion did you enjoy the most? Why?
10. Which chapter was the hardest for you to read?
11. How did discussing the Ten Commandments as Ten Words help in your conversations?
12. Which of the Ten Words would you feel least comfortable discussing in a group like the one in the book? Why?
13. In general, which commandment do you think people are most resistant to keeping? Is it the same for you personally?
14. Which commandment do you think would have the greatest impact on our society if people began to keep it? What might this look like?
15. Of the practices the groups came up with for each Word, which was most helpful to you?
16. After reading this book, has the way you view the Ten Commandments changed? If so, how?

An Excerpt from . . . **Ten**

"Can you believe these idiots?"

The loud exclamation rose above the murmur of early morning conversation in the coffee shop. John, a regular and pastor of a church in the neighborhood, sighed as the serenity of the day's first sip of aromatic coffee was shattered. Looking up, he caught the eye of the man. "OK, Steve, I'll bite. Which particular idiots are we talking about this morning?"

The source of the exclamation, a local business owner, held up the newspaper he had been reading and jabbed a finger at the headline: "Ten Commandments Fight Is Costly," he recited, practically spitting the words out. Some of the other early morning regulars turned their attention toward Steve, anticipating one of his customary rants. He obliged.

"Seems like some good Christian council members in a couple of counties south of here decided the best use of taxpayers' money was to fight the ACLU so they could post copies of the Ten Commandments in their courthouses. They argued all the way up to the Supreme Court and lost, and now they owe the ACLU close to $500,000 in attorney fees." Steve turned back to the paper, "And I quote, 'Officials from the counties admit they do not know how they are going to pay the bill.'" With a snort of disgust he threw the paper down on the table. "What do you think about that, preacher?"

As the attention shifted from Steve to John, he took a long swig of coffee, wondering what it would be like to be able to simply drink a cup of coffee in his neighborhood café without being the resident expert on religion. "Well, why *would* they do that? As a matter of principle?"

"Pretty expensive principle," interjected Steve.

"Indeed. Maybe it was the belief that posting them will keep people on the straight and narrow?"

"But if the first time someone sees them is in a courthouse, don't you think it's a little too late by then?" That got a big laugh from the morning crowd. Steve stood and took a bow. John smiled.

"That's not exactly news, is it?" said someone at the bar. "People are always trying to post the Ten Commandments in public spaces."

“Yeah,” said her companion. “How many millions of dollars have been wasted arguing *that*?”

Jenny, a popular figure in the neighborhood who ran a nonprofit organization working with at-risk youth, jumped in. “Seriously. Those things are thousands of years old. Why does anyone care? It’s not like people still go to church—no offense, John.”

“None taken, Jenny.”

Sam, long-time resident and a deacon in the local Baptist church, piped up from his stool at the bar. “But they’re not just a religious symbol, are they? They’re a pretty weighty cultural symbol—if you’ll excuse my pun.”

One of the baristas leaned around an espresso machine. “I read recently that whenever opinion polls are conducted about the Ten Commandments, 70 to 80 percent of Americans oppose removing them from public display. Yet at the same time only 40 percent of us can name more than four of them.”

The other barista snorted. “Ha! Sounds like we know what they look like, but not what they are. How many could *you* name?” His friend shrugged.

Jenny chimed in again, “If it makes you feel better, I remember watching Stephen Colbert interview some House Representative who was sponsoring a bill to display the Ten Commandments in public buildings. When Colbert asked him to name them, he managed three.”

“You see,” said Steve. “That’s what I’m talking about. Another bunch of do-gooders posturing for their constituents.”

THINGS YOUR MOTHER NEVER TOLD YOU

A Woman's Guide to Sexuality

Kim Gaines Eckert

Why aren't Christian women talking about sex?

In this frank exploration of all aspects of what it means to be a sexual being created by God, psychologist Kim Gaines Eckert explores common myths that we have absorbed from popular culture and distorted religious teaching, such as:

- Sex is god or sex is evil
- Sexuality should not be talked about
- You must experience erotic sexual satisfaction to be fulfilled

This book is your companion into a journey of deeper self-understanding as you explore things you may never have discussed with anyone else.

"Redemptive, wise, practical, honest and tender, this book is a welcome addition to the conversation about women's sexuality."

Sarah Bessey, author of *Jesus Feminist*

"A refreshingly grace-filled and intelligent discussion on the ever-daunting topic of sex. . . . These pages contain a no-nonsense honesty that, if applied, will change our lives and the lives of those we seek to love."

Shayne Moore, author of *Refuse to Do Nothing*

ABOUT THE AUTHOR: Kim Gaines Eckert is a licensed psychologist in Chattanooga, Tennessee, where she maintains a private counseling practice at the Relationship Therapy Center and is the clinical director of the Lee University Play Therapy Center. Kim is a national speaker and has been featured on programs such as Moody Radio's *Prime Time America* and *Midday Connection.*

Follow Kim on Twitter (@kimgaineseckert) and visit drkimeckert.com.

◆ QUESTIONS

1. What is it like for you to talk about sexuality? How difficult or easy is it for you to be honest and forthright with yourself? With the group?
2. What lessons did you learn growing up about what it means to be a girl? As a child, how would you have completed these sentences: "Girls are ______________. Boys are_______________."?
3. Describe your response to the three models of womanhood and identity from chapter 3. In what ways do you identify with the male-centered woman? The female-centered woman? The Christ-centered woman? Where do you primarily find your value and worth?
4. In what ways have you internalized cultural messages about how you should look physically or behave sexually? What practical steps can you take to respond to the negative cultural messages about women and sexuality?
5. If you could ask any question about sexuality, what would it be?
6. What do you think is the appeal for so many women of books such as *Fifty Shades of Grey*?
7. How and when do you feel most powerful? Have you experienced a connection between sex and power? In what ways?
8. Even if sex feels dirty and wrong, the truth is that sex is a good and beautiful gift. What are some things you struggle to believe about sex or yourself that you know to be true in your mind, but you have trouble experiencing emotionally or in your body?
9. When you hear Lisa Williams's story in chapter 9, how does it make you feel? In what ways can you learn from her model and respond in practical ways to needs around you?
10. With which of the myths discussed in the book did you most relate, and how have you observed or experienced them in your own life?
11. Reflect on the idea that sexuality is about learning to receive love. Is it easier for you to give or receive love? What could God teach you through learning to receive love from others?
12. God has work prepared for us to do to help bring others closer to his healing and redemption. What is your next step?

VISIONS OF VOCATION

Common Grace for the Common Good

Steven Garber

2015 Christianity Today Award of Merit

Is it possible to know the world and still love the world?

For decades Steve Garber has come alongside a wide range of people as they seek to make sense of the world and their lives. With him we meet many ordinary people in ordinary places who long for their lives to matter—teachers, political leaders, business owners and more.

Vocation is when we come to know the world in all its joy and pain and still love it. Vocation is following our calling to seek the welfare of the world we live in. And in helping the world to flourish, strangely, mysteriously, we find that we flourish too.

"If I could sit at the feet of anyone to learn about vocation, it would be Steven Garber. Tuck yourself away in a corner with these pages and prepare your heart and soul to dream again."

Gabe Lyons, author of *The Next Christians* and founder, Q Ideas

"Steve Garber has a way of making me feel spiritually rich. What he thinks and says is what I need. . . . Feast on this book and be fed."

Mark Labberton, president, Fuller Theological Seminary

ABOUT THE AUTHOR: Steven Garber is the principal of The Washington Institute for Faith, Vocation & Culture. A consultant to foundations, corporations and schools, he is the author of *The Fabric of Faithfulness* and a contributor to *Faith Goes to Work: Reflections from the Marketplace* and *Get Up Off Your Knees: Preaching the U2 Catalogue*. He lives with his wife, Meg, in Virginia.

◆ QUESTIONS

1. In chapter 1, Steve writes: "This is a book about the most difficult task, the most important task. There is nothing we are asked to do that requires more of us than to know and to love at the same time." Do you agree or disagree and why? Where do you find knowing and loving most challenging in your life right now?
2. What are some obstacles that get in the way of "seeing" properly? What helped Gary Haugen to see clearly enough to found IJM? What contributed to Nazi Adolph Eichmann's failure to see truthfully?
3. In what ways have you felt the numbness Steve describes in chapter 3? What are some of the downsides to living in the information age?
4. "A mind without a heart is nothing" (p. 82). Does this resonate with you? Why or why not?
5. "Relationship, revelation, responsibility" (p. 92). In the Hebrew vision of life, these three are inextricably intertwined. How does the story of the French villagers in Le Chambon-sur-Lignon illustrate this covenantal epistemology? Give an example from your own life where revelation or relationship has led to taking responsibility.
6. Steve argues that "words have to become flesh" and cites several examples of Jesus "incarnating words like holiness and mercy, wisdom and compassion" (p. 125). How might meditating on the Gospels help us to embrace and live into our vocations with more integrity?
7. In chapter 6, Steve gives numerous examples of various couples and individuals who have discovered and pursued their vocations. Which of these stories did you find most compelling, and why?
8. When faced with the challenge of truly engaging in life around you, do you find yourself more tempted toward indulging in stoicism (apathy) or cynicism?
9. Regarding Charles Dickens' *A Christmas Carol*, Steve observes, "the heart of the story is that an ordinary man with an ordinary life saw himself implicated in and through his vocation, and chose to do what he could." How does the story of Ebenezer Scrooge's transformation encourage you as you consider your own vocation?

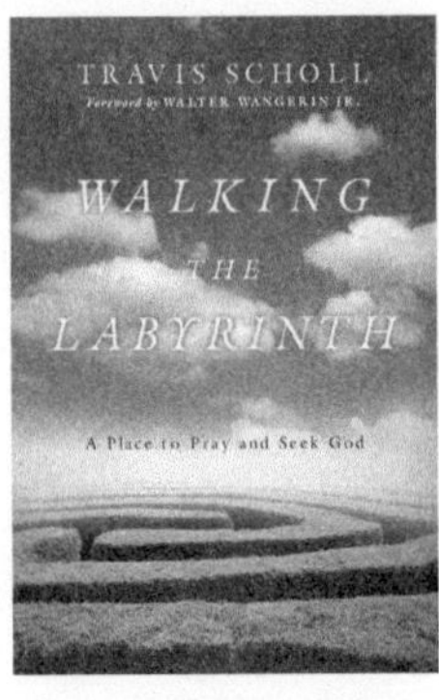

WALKING THE LABYRINTH

A Place to Pray and Seek God

Travis Scholl

Foreword by Walter Wangerin Jr.

One day Travis Scholl discovered a labyrinth in his neighborhood. As he began to walk it, he found this ancient practice offered a much-needed path away from life's demands, allowing him to encounter God in quiet solitude.

With no end, but only a center, labyrinths become a physical symbol of prayer and our journey with God. Each step unites faith and action as travelers take one step at a time, living each moment in trust and willingness to follow the course set before them.

Providing a historical and modern context for this unique spiritual discipline, Scholl weaves his own journey through a labyrinth with the Gospel of Mark's telling of the twists and turns of Jesus' life, providing forty reflections ideal for daily reading during Lent or any time of the year.

"As Travis Scholl invites readers to join him in walking the labyrinth, he guides them not only along a spiraling path on the ground but also on a journey into the heart of Christian faith. Read and walk with him through these pages and discover new paths into Scripture and prayer."

Dorothy C. Bass, author of *Practicing our Faith*

ABOUT THE AUTHOR: Travis Scholl is the managing editor for theological publications at Concordia Seminary in St. Louis. He writes regularly for the *St. Louis Post-Dispatch* on religion and culture and has published poems in *Peregrine, Palimpsest* and *Prospect*. He holds an MDiv from Yale University Divinity School and is ordained in the LCMS. He is also the author of *Living Lent: Daily Prayers for the Season.*

Watch a video about this unique spiritual discipline at ivpress.com/labyrinth.

◆ QUESTIONS

1. Has anyone in your group ever walked this kind of prayer labyrinth (not a maze) before? What was the experience like?
2. Who knows the location of the two or three nearest labyrinths to you? Are you interested in organizing an outing together? Or do you think you'd prefer to go alone?
3. Scholl asks, "What is the center of your life? Have you found it?" (p. 22). Do you like this question? How would you answer it?
4. What have been your own practices of observing the season of Lent? Have they helped you walk more closely with God? What would you recommend to others?
5. Throughout the book, Scholl includes imaginative readings of scenes in Mark. Are there any that struck you as particularly insightful? Any that seemed off the mark? Why?
6. Scholl includes a prayer, "O God, you have called your servants to ventures of which we cannot see the ending, by paths as yet untrodden, through perils unknown" (p. 92). What are some of the ventures like these in your life? What "paths" do you hope for? What "perils" do you fear?
7. Does Scholl's acceptance of the repetitiveness of the labyrinth, its intentional lack of progress and its slowness frustrate you or seem pointless? What are some things you think you need to be advancing toward?
8. Scholl concludes the book, writing of the resurrected Jesus, "He is going ahead. I am chasing after. With each step, we are gaining ground to meet him" (p. 230). In what ways would you say you're "gaining ground" and getting closer to Christ?
9. Pick a passage you like and then read it aloud with your group. Do you think it makes a difference to hear the text out loud versus silently reading this book to yourself?
10. What kind of person would benefit the most from this book?

An Excerpt from . . . **Walking the Labyrinth**

There are infinite ways to walk the labyrinth.

Such is the ancient, worldwide story of the labyrinth.

But how does the labyrinth become a personal story? How did it become *my* story?

The story of the labyrinth became my story by way of pilgrimage and prayer. Or, perhaps, I became part of its story. I pray its path. Its path makes of me a prayer.

When we think of prayer, we think of words, of a conversation. Indeed prayer is this. But the labyrinth, as a discipline of prayer, is an *act* of prayer. In the labyrinth I pray by taking each next step, one foot in front of the other. The labyrinth makes of prayer an act, and it makes of action a prayer. In it, word and act are united, made one.

When I was little, this is how I was taught to pray: to close my eyes, bow my head, fold my hands. Then to speak into thin air. This is true. This is a way to pray. And yet the labyrinth is a physical reminder, a sign, that prayer is also a place, a space in which life—new life—is lived.

Prayer is not the thin air of a void.

Prayer is the world made out of the void, in word and action.

And isn't that what prayer is, after all, the making one of time and space, speaking and action, walk and talk, in the life of faith? After all is said and done, isn't prayer the uniting of one's life by listening to the voice of the One unseen, the One who kills and makes alive by one spoken word?

Oddly enough, this makes the labyrinth—the place of solitude—a place of encounter.

I walk the labyrinth in solitude but never alone.

This is the mystery of the presence of Christ in the world. Christ sits at the right hand of God, to recall Martin Luther, because the right hand of God is the whole cosmos, this earth, everything within it.

The One unseen becomes the One seen in all creation.

This becomes its next paradox: the path of the labyrinth is a process of encounter. This is paradox, because it is a solitary journey. Nevertheless, it is a journey to the center of things, of life, of my own identity, perhaps even into all reality.

It is a journey into an encounter with God in Jesus Christ.

And if the right hand of God is the whole cosmos, then all of life can be a labyrinth.

And in that singular encounter with the One who sits at the center of all life and all reality, I walk into ever new discoveries of who I am and how I am to live in the worlds in which God has set me—home, neighborhood, work, family, ad infinitum. And I am transformed by the encounter.

But how does the labyrinth—these thin circles of brick in grass—do all these things?

More to the point: How can I walk the labyrinth as a path to all these discoveries? I know of only one way to answer the question. And the answer is even easier than it sounds.

By taking the first step.

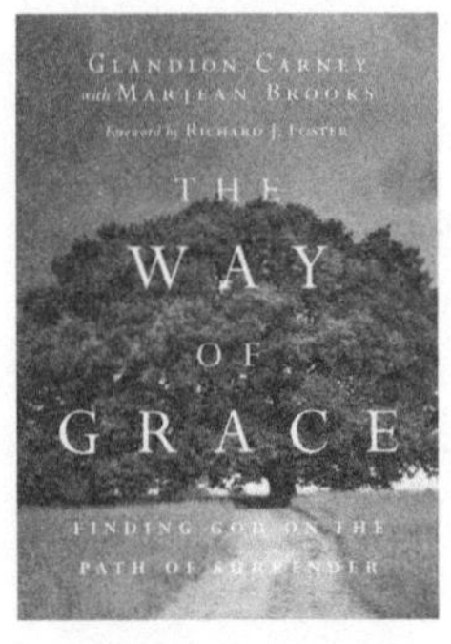

THE WAY OF GRACE

Finding God on the Path of Surrender

Glandion Carney with Marjean Brooks

Foreword by Richard J. Foster

"No matter how old you are or how many degrees you have or don't have—when grace takes you to school, you start in kindergarten."

This was the experience of Reverend Glandion Carney when he was given the life-altering news that he has Parkinson's disease. This was not supposed to be his journey. How could he face it?

With poignant vulnerability, *The Way of Grace* describes one man's journey into a new land of God's amazing grace. Both his honesty and his resilience will inspire and inform your own times of difficulty.

God's unmerited grace saves us, strengthens us and sanctifies us. We too can experience lives full of grace and truth, courageously searching out God's wonders every day.

"For some, receiving the dreaded diagnosis of Parkinson's would be a death knell, but for my friend Glandion, it became the occasion to ring a different bell, and to mine his own soul for lessons of grace."

Gary W. Moon, executive director of the Dallas Willard Center

"Anyone facing a seeming debilitating transition or walking alongside that person needs Glandion at their side, telling them both the truths and stories contained in this marvelous book."

Jan Johnson, author of *Abundant Simplicity*

ABOUT THE AUTHOR: The Reverend Glandion Carney was associate pastor of pastoral care at St. Peter's Anglican Church in Birmingham, Alabama, until his recent retirement from active ministry. He was involved in Renovaré for fifteen years and was chaplain of the Christian Legal Society. Glandion and his wife Marion life in Birmingham where he enjoys volunteering with the Parkinson's Foundation.

◆ QUESTIONS

1. Glandion describes his reaction to receiving his Parkinson's diagnosis. He explains that it was easier to live in denial than to do the hard work of acceptance. Why do you think acceptance is hard work? Or does it come easy to you?

2. Focusing on the physical challenges of the disease prevents Glandion from joining in the mystical experience of the Eucharist. Once he submits to Jesus, he becomes more aware of Jesus' presence. How does Glandion's example of submission help in understanding Christian submission in everyday life?

3. The grace of relinquishment required Glandion to give up responsibilities he enjoyed. Were you surprised by his anger? How might this step be more difficult than acceptance and submission? What would be hardest for you to give up due to physical limitation?

4. Glandion shares a story of a woman who offers to carry his luggage. He declines but she doesn't give up. Would you have had the gumption to insist on helping someone? Why is it often harder to receive compassion than extend it?

5. Self-pity and feelings of abandonment from God cause Glandion to turn to alcohol. Eventually he shared his struggles with friends. Do you think it's possible to recover from addiction and spiritual crisis alone? How can we make it easier for those in need to turn to a friend?

6. The grace of comfort is "knowing that God is faithful while learning to be alone and quiet with him" (p. 100). When have you experienced comfort from God?

7. "Grace doesn't flow by *adding* more to our lives; instead it fills the places where we have *subtracted* extraneous elements" (p. 117). What can you subtract from your life to let the spirit fill?

8. Glandion writes, "In order to experience true hope, I had to walk through complete hopelessness" (p. 126). What do you think he means by this?

9. Of all the graces Glandion writes about—acceptance, submission, relinquishment, compassion, trust, community, comfort and hope —which do you need most in your life today?

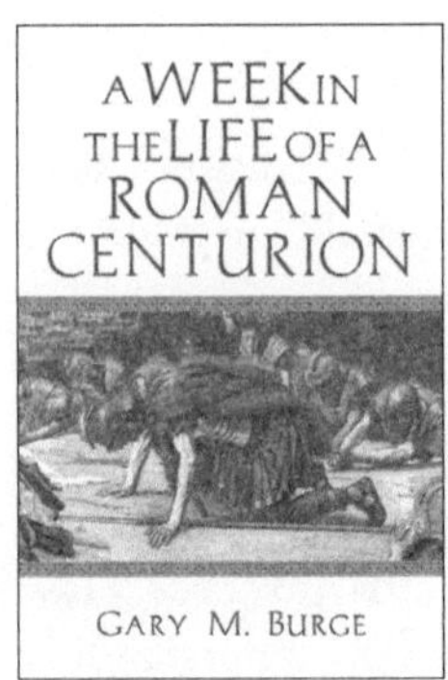

A WEEK IN THE LIFE OF A ROMAN CENTURION

Gary M. Burge

Enter a world of warfare and treachery, of duty and honor, of love and loyalty, interwoven with the inner workings of a Roman centurion's household. And then trace it as the road curves toward little Capernaum.

Follow the story of Appius, a proud centurion, and Tullus, his scribe and slave. From a battle with the Parthians, through a tragic personal crisis, to the gladiator arena at Caesarea Maritima, their tale finally leads to the backwater village of Capernaum on the shores of Galilee. There, in a culture not their own and during a week they will never forget, they encounter a Jewish prophet from Nazareth. In entertaining historical fiction, splashed with informative sidebars and images, we capture a view of Jesus' world from the outer framework looking in.

"Masterfully written and extensively researched, this fast-paced account invites the reader into the first-century world of the Gospels even while intriguing the reader as a good story should."

Craig Keener, Asbury Theological Seminary

"Biblical scholars are not typically known for writing historical novels, much less gripping page-turners. Gary Burge, however, has accomplished both of these feats."

Craig L. Blomberg, Denver Seminary

ABOUT THE AUTHOR: Gary M. Burge (PhD, University of Aberdeen) is professor of New Testament at Wheaton College in Wheaton, Illinois. His passion in teaching, research and writing is how the unique world of the Middle East in antiquity shapes how we read the New Testament today. He is the author, co-author or editor of *Theology Questions Everyone Asks, The Baker Illustrated Bible Commentary, The New Testament in Antiquity, John: The Gospel of Life* and *Whose Land? Whose Promise?*

◆ QUESTIONS

1. How is Appius different from the other Roman military leaders, especially in the way he treats his slaves Tullus, Gaius and Livia?
2. The Roman way, the *Via Romana*, was a life carefully built around values of honor, strength and discipline (chap. 4). What are some negative and positive consequences of this ideology? Do you see these values reflected in society today?
3. When Tullus meets the Jewish village elders, they help him reconnect to the Jewish faith of his family (pp. 133-134). What do you think Tullus was feeling as he explored that faith? Can you point to a time in your own life when you experienced a reconnection to your faith?
4. When Tobias and Miriam are asked to enter Appius's Roman villa to help Livia during childbirth (pp. 136-138), how does each of them react? How do their religious beliefs affect their actions? How does your religion affect your interactions with those with different belief systems?
5. How does Appius attempt to keep the peace with the village elders (p. 154)? Why did he use this strategy instead of the traditional Roman show of force? Which is more successful?
6. Identify turning points in the story for each of the main characters. Why were these moments significant?
7. Discuss the women in the story, Livia and Miriam. How are they the same? How are they different? What draws them together? What affect does each of them have on Appius's life?
8. Why do you think Jesus chose to ignore Jewish law when he healed a Roman servant and entered a Roman household?
9. What is so powerful about the scene where Appius and Jesus talk in the garden (pp. 187-189)? How does this relate to your own experience?
10. How is Jesus portrayed in the story? How does this compare with your perception of Jesus?
11. What do you think happens next in the story for Appius, Tullus and the rest of the characters? See the author's prediction on page 191.
12. This is a fictional account of the story found in Matthew 8:5-13 and Luke 7:1-10. How has reading this book given you insight into those Bible passages?

WHAT YOUR BODY KNOWS ABOUT GOD

How We Are Designed to Connect, Serve and Thrive

Rob Moll
Foreword by Michael Card

Our bodies have actually been created to love God and serve our neighbors.

Award-winning journalist Rob Moll reports on neuroscience findings that show how our brains actually change and adapt when engaged in spiritual practices. God has created our bodies to fulfill the Great Commandment; we are hardwired to commune with God and to have community with other people.

Rob explores the neuroscience of prayer, how liturgy helps us worship, why loving God causes us to love others, and how a life of love and service leads to the abundant life for which we were created. Heighten your spiritual senses and discover how you have been designed for physical and spiritual flourishing.

"Thank God, he has made us for glory that extends to the tips of our toes and even to our neural pathways. Read this and let your whole self rejoice."

Katelyn Beaty, managing editor, *Christianity Today* magazine

"Got a body? Wanna love God? Then this is your book, which means it is my book and everyone's book. . . . Our bodies are not a curse but a gift."

Leslie Leyland Fields, author of *Forgiving Our Fathers and Mothers*

ABOUT THE AUTHOR: Rob Moll is an award-winning journalist and editor-at-large with *Christianity Today.* He has written extensively on health and health-care issues, investing and personal finance, religion and rural America. His work has appeared in the *Wall Street Journal, Profitable Investing, Books & Culture* and *Leadership*. Rob serves World Vision as communications officer to the president and lives in the Seattle area.

◆ QUESTIONS

1. After reading, did you feel more aware of how you physically respond to worship and prayer? Can you name any specific examples?
2. How does the examination of Psalm 139 in the foreword set the stage for the rest of the book? How does Rob's writing model that psalm?
3. The author writes in chapter 2 that "children need formative connections with other people, and they expect to discover God." How have you seen this play out with young children in your life?
4. Rob writes in chapter 5, "They often say that for the brain, falling in love is similar to a hit of cocaine.... Human beings from biblical times to today have related to God as a lover. The analogy isn't simply an attempt to compare two intense kinds of relationships. We use this language of love and union because that's how it feels to be absorbed in our experience of God." Can you relate to the description?
5. When the author talks about his wife Clarissa's struggle with anxiety, how did that make you feel about the goodness of God?
6. In chapter 8, the author discusses the ways in which our brain processes worship. Take a moment to examine the worship experiences in which you feel all the senses. What do they include? How can you duplicate those experiences outside of Sunday morning service?
7. What are some ways you can put into practice the research the author unveils in chapter 9, "Acts of Service"? How did this chapter inspire you to reach out in your community as a way of worship?
8. How did you feel about this book in light of our ever busy and ever connected culture? Did the author's words inspire you to slow down and listen? Describe your experience of this.
9. After reading this book, how have you noticed that your faith experiences and personal health are tied together?
10. "The Christian way heals, provides meaning, gives hope and offers a path to a good life by connecting us to God and other people," Rob writes in chapter 12. How can you use this book and the research the author provided to reach out to non-Christian friends and family?

Taken from . . . **What Your Body Knows About God**

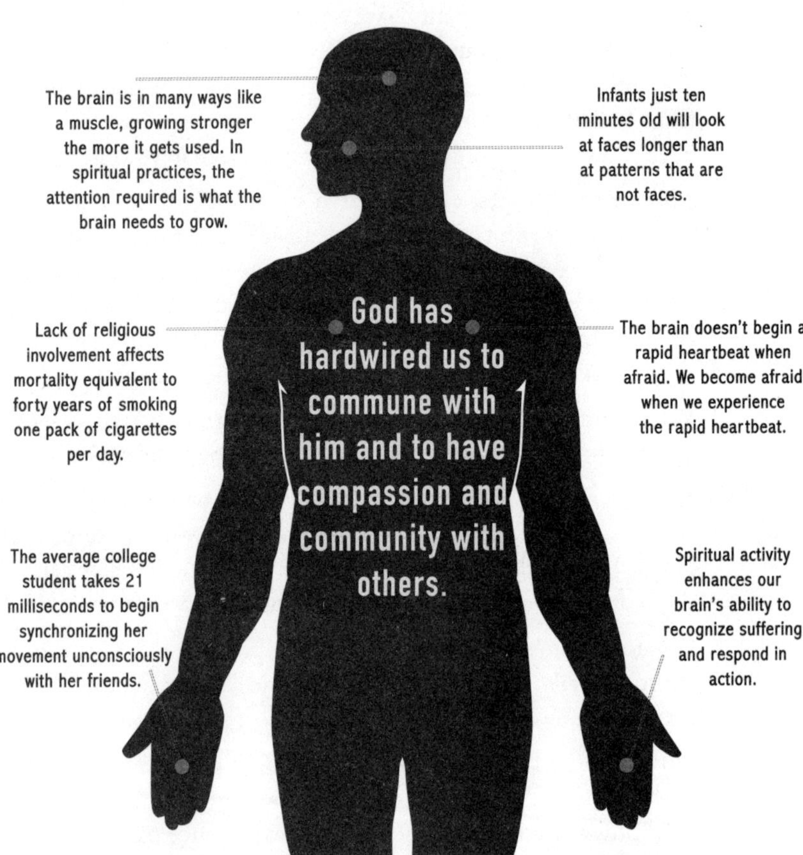

LEADING A BOOK DISCUSSION

Discussing a book in a group can help clarify any questions readers have as well as sharpen what response is appropriate. The questions for each title assume that participants have read the book. You may want to mention this to your group before you select a book for discussion.

For the leader:

Read the book carefully and mark it up well. Note your own questions or responses.

You don't want to be overbearing, nor do you want to be passive. Your goal is to help the group flourish in its understanding and application of the book, not impress people with how much you know.

In addition to the specific book questions, leaders may also ask questions like, "What parts of this chapter struck you the most? Did you underline or highlight anything that was particularly meaningful to you?"

Additional guidelines to help you:

- At the beginning of your first time together, explain that these studies are meant to be discussions, not lectures. Encourage the members of the group to participate. However, do not put pressure on those who may be hesitant to speak.
- Begin each study on time.
- The study questions are designed to be read aloud just as they are written. You may, however, prefer to express them in your own words.
- Note also that there may be times when it is appropriate to deviate from the discussion guide. For example, a question may have already been answered. If so, move on to the next question. Or someone may raise an important question not covered in the guide. Take time to discuss it, but try to keep the group from going off on tangents.
- Avoid answering your own questions. An eager group quickly becomes passive and silent if members think the leader will do most of the talking. If necessary, repeat or rephrase the question

until it is clearly understood, or refer to the commentary woven into the guide to clarify the context or meaning.

- Don't be afraid of silence in response to the discussion questions. People may need time to think about the question before formulating their answers.
- Don't be content with just one answer. Ask, "What do the rest of you think?" or "Anything else?" until several people have given answers to the question.
- Try to be affirming whenever possible. Especially affirm participation. Never reject an answer; if it seems clearly off-base, ask, "What led you to that conclusion?" or again, "What do the rest of you think?"
- Don't expect every answer to be addressed to you, even though this will probably happen at first. As group members become more at ease, they will begin to truly interact with each other. This is one sign of healthy discussion.
- Don't be afraid of controversy. It can be very stimulating. If you don't resolve an issue completely, don't be frustrated. Explain that the group will move on and God may enlighten all of you in later sessions.
- Periodically summarize what the group has said. This helps to draw together the various ideas mentioned and gives continuity to the study. But don't preach.
- End on time.

BOOKS DELIVERED TO YOUR DOOR EVERY MONTH

IVP Book Club

The hardest part about being an IVP Book Club member is choosing from the many great books we offer. The rest is easy!

How the Club Works

To join, choose three of our specially selected books and get them for just $1 each. Once you receive your three books, you'll be sent our monthly Book Club Digest with information on the Main Selection, plus many other titles to choose from. If you want the Main Selection that month, do nothing. If we don't hear from you by the specified date, we will automatically ship it to you.

As a member, you get a 30 percent discount off the retail price of any book you purchase at any time—ebooks too! If you wish to order another book from the Digest, or you don't want any of the selections, simply indicate it on the reply card and return it to us before the date shown. And you can always respond online at ivpbookclub.com.

Get Started

Choose your first three books, and we'll send them to you for only $1 each plus postage and handling. Then let the reading begin!

Join today at ivpbookclub.com/join

Browse and Buy Ebooks from IVP

We've got more than 1,000 ebooks available at ivpress.com.

When you buy an ebook from IVP, you get it in every format we offer—typically epub, mobi and PDF. We sell unrestricted, DRM-free ebook file formats so that you can easily transfer titles to all of your personal apps and devices. See each book's web page for details.

Recent Digital Book World's QED Seal Award Winners

For a complete list of ebooks visit
ivpress.com/ebooks

Subscribe to the **IVP Ebooks Update** and receive word via email whenever we release a fresh batch of ebooks.

FOLLOW AND SHARE!

MORE BOOK DISCUSSION GUIDES:

www.ivpress.com/**readup**

FACEBOOK:

www.facebook.com/**intervarsitypress**

TWITTER:

@ivpress

YOUTUBE:

www.youtube.com/**intervarsitypress**

GOODREADS:

http://bit.ly/**ivpgoodreads**

SCRIBD:

www.scribd.com/**InterVarsityPress**